McAfee Anti-Virus for Beginners

Abacus

Table Of Contents

5. McAfee's VirusShield 83

6. WebScan And Other Internet Protection 101

Table Of Contents

Using The Companion CD-ROM

Chapter 1

What's In This Chapter

Using The Companion CD-ROM

To use the companion CD-ROM, you must first load the MENU.EXE program located in the root directory of the CD. When this program is loaded, you will have various buttons for selecting your utilities.

Insert the CD-ROM into your CD-ROM drive. We're assuming in this chapter that the letter assigned to your CD-ROM drive is "D:". If this is not the case, simply substitute your CD-ROM drive letter instead of "D:".

THE MENU PROGRAM

Loading the MENU in Windows 3.x

Select the **File/Run...** command in the Windows Program Manager:

This opens the Run dialog box. Then type the following in the Run dialog box:

```
d:\menu.exe
```

The Run dialog box should now look like the following:

Then press the ⌜Enter⌟ key or click the ⌜OK⌟ button. The main MENU program will start. This MENU program is used to install or test various shareware utilities.

Loading the MENU program in Win 95

Select the Start menu and then the **Run...** command. This opens the Run dialog box. Type the following in the Run dialog box:

```
d:\menu.exe
```

The Run dialog box should now look like the following:

Now press the [Enter] key or click the [OK] button. The main MENU program will start. This MENU program is used to install or test various shareware utilities.

The Main Menu screen

Installing Adobe's Acrobat Reader

Adobe's Acrobat Reader is a utility allowing you to view PDF files. Two PDF files are available on the companion CD-ROM:

1. BOOKFILE.PDF

2. CATALOG.PDF

Installing Adobe's Acrobat Reader

If you already have Acrobat Reader, skip the next steps and go on to the other notes. Follow these steps to install Acrobat Reader on your hard drive (requires approximately 2 Meg on space on your hard drive). Insert the CD-ROM in your drive and load Windows. Run D:\ACROREAD.EXE from the Windows Program Manager.

Simply follow the instructions and prompts which appear on your screen. Double click the Acrobat Reader icon to load it. After Acrobat Reader is loaded, select the **File/Open...** command and select MAINFILE.PDF to view and read McAfee Anti-Virus for Beginners directly on your PC screen.

Installing WinZip

WinZip is a very handy tool for working with compressed files. The latest version is 6.2. It also lets you link your virus scanning software to scan zipped files before extracting or executing them.

Installing Niko Mak Computing's WinZip

To install an evaluation version of WinZip, click its button in the main menu and follow the instructions. Read Chapter 6 and the documents included with WinZip to learn more about how to use the features of the program.

Installing EZ Download

EZ Download automates the difficult or tedious steps of downloading files from the Internet and world wide web. You may also link a web-enabled virus scanner to it to scan incoming files for viruses before they can infect your system. To install an evaluation version of EZ Download, click its button on the main menu of the CD-ROM and follow the on-screen instructions. Read chapter six and the included EZ Download documents for more information on using EZ Download.

Installing EZ Download

Installing McAfee Anti-Virus evaluation version

McAfee's VirusScan is the leading anti-virus program in the world. So you may follow the examples in the book and try out VirusScan's features, McAfee consented to let us provide you with an evaluation version of VirusScan. To install the program, click the McAfee button in the main menu of the CD-ROM. For more information on using VirusScan, read the rest of this book and the included document files from McAfee.

COMPANION CD-ROM PROGRAM NOTES

The programs featured on the CD-ROM are fully functioning *shareware evaluation versions* of the best programs available today. Shareware benefits both the user and the author. By avoiding distribution, packaging, and advertising costs, prices of shareware remain low.

Keep in mind, however, that shareware programs are copyrighted programs, not freeware. Therefore, the authors (McAfee & Associates, MMMMM Software, Inc. and Niko Mak Computing, Inc.) require payment if you continue using their program(s) after a specified trial period. This lets you try out the program for a limited time, typically 30 days, and should give you enough time to decide whether you want to keep the program. If you continue to use the program, you're required to send the author a nominal fee. Please read the README.1ST in this directory for instructions.

After registration you will frequently get the current full version of the program without restrictions and shareware notes, as well as the option of purchasing upgraded versions later for a reduced price. As a rule, larger applications include a users manual. Shareware programs usually feature the complete performance range of the full versions. Some programs use special messages to indicate they're shareware versions. The message usually appears immediately after program startup or can be called from the Help menu.

The companion CD-ROM shows the variety of shareware available. To ensure that the program authors continue writing programs and offering them as shareware, we urge you to support the shareware concept by registering the programs that you plan to use permanently.

You'll find program instructions and notes on registration for the shareware programs in special text files located in the program directory of each program. These programs are usually called READ.ME, README.TXT or README.DOC. As a rule, the TXT, WRI or DOC extensions are used for text files, which you can view and print with Windows 95 editors.

The MENU program is a component of the companion CD-ROM. It's not shareware, freeware or public domain. Please do not redistribute the MENU program from Abacus.

9

Introduction

Chapter 2

2

What's In This Chapter

Introduction

Over 100 new computer viruses are detected each month. They travel by floppy diskettes, bulletin boards, E-mail attachments, networks and the Internet. The result of infection can range from a virus displaying an annoying but basically harmless smiley face and message on your monitor to a virus that completely wipes out all the data on your hard drive.

What are the chances of your computer system becoming infected with a virus? No one can say for certain. However, keep in mind that you run the risk of infecting your computer each time you run a new program, enter new data into memory, copy files onto your hard drive or read from an unfamiliar diskette.

Avoiding infection is difficult. The only sure way is to turn your computer off and leave it off. But that is not a practical solution for most users. Education and virus-hunting software are much better alternatives for virus prevention and detection.

McAfee's VirusScan and WebScan are the leading Virus protection programs for the PC and web browsing. Combined with user awareness, these programs will detect and clean infections on your machine and prevent others from getting into your system. To understand how they do this, you should understand what a virus is and how it spreads.

MAKEUP OF A VIRUS

Computer viruses have similarities to biological viruses (see the following table).

Function	Biological viruses	Computer viruses
Attacks/Infects	Specific body cells	Specific programs (all COM or EXE programs, etc.)
Purpose	Modify the genetic codes of a cell other than the original.	Manipulate the data in the program.
Replication	New viruses grow in the infected cell itself.	The infected program produces other infected programs.
Re-infection	An infected cell is not infected more than once.	A program is infected only once by most viruses.
Incubation period	Symptoms may not appear for a long time.	The infected program can work without error for an extended time.
Other similarities	Organism may develop immunity to the virus. Viruses can mutate and therefore cannot be clearly told apart.	Programs can be made immune to the virus. Virus programs escape detection by modifying themselves.

However, a computer virus is not bacterial or alive. An electronic virus is a string of computer code (a program) that can make a copy of itself. It attempts to attach itself to boot, executable or data files and modify the host program, replicating itself in the process and potentially damaging files used by the host program or system.

When a virus program is started, it searches the current drive for a user program it can modify (infect). When the virus finds a such a program, it tests the program to determine if it has already been infected. When a virus infects a program, it places a marker byte in that program. This marker byte is a footprint that indicates the virus is already present. A virus looks for this marker so it won't reinfect a program already carrying the virus. If the reintroduced virus finds this marker, it skips this program and moves on to the next, again looking for its signature marker.

If the second program is uninfected and a program type that the virus can infect, then the virus inserts its kernel into the program. It does this by overwriting the start of the program on the disk drive with a copy of itself. It then discreetly labels the program with its marker. You may notice write only access to the disk drive as the virus spreads.

When this second program is started, the virus program is executed because it overwrote the original programing code. The virus then reproduces itself again in the same way in the third user program. Because a part of the original program code was deleted to make way for the virus, program errors may be noticed after the virus copies itself.

For a program to be commonly defined as a virus it must meet the following criteria:

❖ Be able to replicate itself

❖ Modify software not belonging to the virus program by binding its program structures into this software.

❖ Be capable of executing the modification on several programs.

❖ Recognize the modification performed on a program.

❖ Be able to prevent further modification of the same program upon such recognition.

While viruses can do real damage to your data, the most threatening aspect of viruses is that they develop a sort of life of their own. The author has only limited, if any, control over the program. Once sent into a computing environment, viruses are controlled only by their programming, and leave only a sketchy trail, at best. Also, anyone developing viruses for criminal purposes has only a small risk of being caught. It's nearly impossible to determine the origin of viral programs once they are in a network. Added to this is the fact that a carrier program can be removed from the system after being started without breaking the chain of infection. A person writing a virus program can, with some care, completely hide his or her trail.

Furthermore, viruses are no longer restrained to floppy diskettes passed hand-to-hand or to direct PC to PC connections via modems or serial links. Computer viruses can spread very quickly through Local Area Networks; the World Wide Web allows viruses anywhere in the world to be downloaded by unsuspecting surfers.

2 Introduction

Parts of a virus

Most viruses have the following four main parts:

Replicator

The replicator contains code for attaching to another program and copying the virus.

Protector

The protector hides the virus from detection, usually with encryption or polymorphing. Encrypting viruses try to hide by encoding themselves or the infected program into a format unrecognized by scanning software. Polymorphous viruses alter their internal structure or encrypting techniques with each infection to keep from being identified by a signature code. These viruses contain several individual pieces of executable code (and often null-code, non-active fillers) that can be rearranged into any order, and so their code is unique to each infection.

Trigger

The trigger is an event for which the virus is programmed to watch. It tells the virus when to detonate, on a certain date, when a certain application is launched or keystroke combination is entered, for example. When the trigger activates the virus, its payload is detonated.

Payload

The payload is what happens upon detonation. This may be simple replication, a one time message, an annoying beep on every keystroke, or massive data loss, as examples. The majority of viruses merely replicate.

The complexity of these various parts differs among the viruses, based on the ability and purpose(s) of the author. The more successful viruses have elaborate protection schemes to avoid detection and payloads that are more subtle than those that create great havoc. If the goal of a virus author is to propagate the virus, it makes no sense to kill the host, or even let it know that a virus is present.

AREAS THAT VIRUSES ATTACK

Viruses can not attack your computer indiscriminately. Only three areas of your computer system are vulnerable to viruses. Unfortunately, three is more than enough.

Many viruses attack and travel in floppy disk boot sectors. Even more attach to executable program files. And there is a growing class of viruses that take advantage of the macro language used in some larger applications.

Boot sectors

About two hundred viruses hide in the boot sector of floppy disks and infect a computer when it is booted from an infected disk. These account for eighty to ninety percent of widespread infections. The boot sector is loaded into memory first, before virus protection code can be executed, and contains your computer's instructions for starting up. Boot sector viruses interfere when you turn on or reboot your system, and may infect other floppies used on the infected system. These can also infect your system when an infected disk is accessed after booting and the virus moves into memory. Boot sector viruses can't infect across a network or via downloaded files.

Files

File infector viruses attach to executable files (.EXE, .COM, .DLL, etc.) by overwriting part of the original programming code. When the host program is executed, the virus's code is run instead of that of the original program. It then infects other applications the user accesses by hiding in the computer's memory. Turning off the computer (a cold boot) will eliminate the virus in memory. However, it will remain in infected programs and will return to memory when one of these is executed. Virus scanning software can clean most infected files so they can be safely used again.

The following lists the file types attacked by file infector viruses:

❖ 386	❖ BIN	❖ COM	❖ DLL	❖ DRV
❖ EXE	❖ FON	❖ OVL	❖ SYS	❖ VXD

Macro data files

The third type are macro viruses. First encountered in late 1995, these are the first viruses to spread across operating systems. They accomplish this by infecting data files of programs that use macro languages to automate repetitive tasks. Word and Excel are two examples of programs with macro languages. These are particularly infectious because they do not need an explicit command to activate. They execute when a document is opened or closed, or they observe another action for which the authors programmed the viruses to watch. Once running, macro viruses can infect other documents, delete files and create problems in your system. When a Word.macro virus is activated, it copies itself to the global normal.dot template, and so becomes available to all open documents. Fortunately, most of these viruses are quite limited in the damage they can do, relative to the others.

Memory resident viruses, a subset of any of these three types, travel by way of floppies, downloads and E-mail attachments (although not E-mail itself). They reside in the computer's memory, causing havoc with valid memory resident programs and infecting others which access the memory.

Multipartite viruses infect diskette boot sectors, the master boot records of hard drives and program files. Because they infect all these areas multipartite viruses spread further and are trickier to remove than other viruses.

HOW DO I CATCH A VIRUS?

Any time you share information between computers you run the risk of acquiring a virus. They travel in the boot sector of floppy disks, in programs and files and in electronic mail attachments, and can be accidentally retrieved from networks, online services, and the Internet.

Floppy disks carry about 200 known viruses which account for roughly three-quarters of all viral infections. The files for starting your PC are in your hard drive's boot sector, and the information in a floppy's boot sector give the computer instructions on reading the disk. When you copy the contents of a disk with an infected boot sector or if you boot from an infected disk, the virus then contaminates your system. These viruses can only travel via floppy disks. You can't get one through a network or download.

File infector viruses attach themselves to executable files. When you run an infected program the virus moves into RAM, infecting other programs you run while it is resident in memory. These viruses can be transferred in floppies, by downloading files or programs from the Internet or across a local network and in E-mail attachments. These viruses are dormant until the contaminated program is executed. Whenever you get a new file or E-mail attachment, run it through a virus scan before opening or executing it. If a virus is found, you can remove the program or file before it infects other components in your system. Most large-site infections are caused by file infecting viruses that are placed on multiple workstations by diskettes and networks.

Macro viruses hide in macro language scripting tools used to automate tedious tasks. The auto-execute macros don't need an explicit command to execute. Viruses can take advantage of these automated commands to set themselves to automatically infect documents as you work. Most users don't think to scan data files like Microsoft Word documents, making them a safe place for viruses to hide. Though these viruses are usually restricted in how far they can penetrate your system, their ability to cross platforms and the wide use of programs using macro languages helps spread these viruses quickly.

Detecting and removing viruses

How do you know if you've contracted a virus? Viruses are programmed to be as stealthy as possible until they're triggered. If a virus announces itself to you, then it's already done its work. A virus will leave certain indications of an infection before it is triggered, but only a programmer who has deciphered the internal structure of the virus can positively identify these. This isn't much help for the average user.

Subtle symptoms of infection do arise, however, because of compatibility problems. Even legitimate computer programs are not always 100% bug-free. Many popular programs and even operating systems have had problems executing properly. Computer virus programs are no different. Furthermore, since most viruses aren't thoroughly tested before their release, they often contain errors or incomplete segments.

These errors create the compatibility problems that provide clues to the existence of viruses. While these may arise for reasons other than virus infection, scan your software if you notice one or more of the following, particularly if you haven't intentionally modified your software recently.

1. Programs execute slower than normally.

2. Programs perform disk access which they didn't before.

3. Load time increases.

4. Obscure system crashes.

5. Programs which could previously be loaded now terminate with the error message "Not enough memory".

6. Increasing storage requirements of programs.

7. Unknown or unclear error messages.

8. Decreasing storage space on the disk without files having been added or expanded.

9. Memory-resident software run with errors or not at all.

10. Executable files unexpectedly vanishing.

11. Workstations unexpectedly rebooting, especially a relatively constant amount of time after being turned on.

12. Unusual displays, including strange messages or icons.

13. An unusually heavy load on a local network or other communication link.

14. Outgoing mail or links to other information that were not intentionally established.

If you suspect a virus has infected your files or system you should immediately switch off your computer. Next, restart your computer from a clean, write-protected boot disk (the emergency start disk in Windows 95, for example, or a backup you've made for just such an emergency).

Use an anti-virus program to locate and repair infected files. The files may be too damaged to be repaired. If this is the case, consider them to be corrupted and replace them with clean copies (remember those backups you had the foresight to make).

Run your anti-virus program a second time, just to be safe. If the anti-virus program still detects a virus or other problem, call technical support for your system or anti-virus software.

Non-viral Computer Ills

As mentioned, many of the symptoms listed above can arise from causes other than virus infections.

Bugs

When complicated, sophisticated software is run on sophisticated, complicated operating systems, minor incompatibilities create clashes that can result in data loss or system crashes that are not related to viruses.

False alarms

Virus protection programs can produce false alarms. A scanner looking for bits of signature code may find a string it recognizes in legitimate programming code, or a checksummer may raise an alert for actions it can't explain, modified file size, for example, that have legitimate causes. If the program marks only one file (that you haven't put at risk lately) as infected, can't name the virus, or identifies it as a virus no longer in the wild, it's likely that your red flag is a red herring. But to be safe, you should always assume an alert is genuine until you learn more about the incident.

Malfunctions

Hardware, the software that controls it and the people who create both are not infallible. If your mouse acts up, your system hangs, you have trouble playing sound or experience most of the other things that can (and do) go wrong with computers, you are more likely to have a malfunction or system conflict than a virus infection.

Practical jokes

Practical jokers sometimes modify computer systems or insert programs to make minor adjustments to a system's functions. Others are rumor mongers, forecasting doom from a mythical virus, like the Good Times hoax. These "jokes" are irksome and unethical, but won't harm your system or programs.

Rabbits

Rabbits have one thing in common with their rodent namesakes—rapid reproduction. Computer rabbits don't infect other programs, and so aren't technically viruses, but they do replicate, on a damaging order of magnitude. The purpose of a rabbit is to reproduce without limit in order to exhaust the resources of a computer system, eventually causing it to freeze and/or crash. Because they don't infect other programs, rabbits won't harm your data. After the rabbit is purged from your system, you can safely use all your files without having to restore them from backups. One of the better known rabbit epidemics originated from Cornell University in November of 1988. It was an accident, an experiment run without adequate supervision, and it crashed most of the computers attached to the Internet.

Trojan horses

A Trojan horse, like the original, is a danger disguised as a gift. Though disguised as an innocuous program or file, Trojan horses often carry a payload that is deadly to your system or files. Trojan horses don't reproduce, and so aren't technically viruses. A well-known Trojan horse was distributed to approximately 20,000 users in 1989 dressed as a health information diskette that was decidedly unhealthy for the users' hard drives. The two styles of Trojan horses are time bombs (triggered by a certain date or time) and logic bombs (triggered by a command entered by an unsuspecting user). Since they can't replicate, Trojan horses are pretty rare

Protection Strategies

Chapter 3

3

What's In This Chapter

Protection Strategies

Computer viruses are a real threat but you don't have to be a victim. Several strategies are available that you can use to protect your computer system against traditional and Internet-savvy viruses.

Protection when using diskettes

The simplest protection is to avoid using unknown diskettes. Most viruses are transported through diskettes that are used on different systems. Whenever you receive a diskette, regardless of the source, make certain it's not carrying a virus. You can do this by scanning it with a virus-protection program.

You should also write-protect your diskettes. Slide the tab in the corner so the window is open. This will prevent any new information from being written onto the diskette, including viruses.

Protection when using CD-ROMs

Since CD-ROMs are a read-only format, they're unlikely to pose a threat of infecting your system. However, even CD-ROMs have carried viruses before. The best policy is to exercise caution and judgment with any new CD-ROMs. This is true with CD-ROMs from manufacturers, too.

3 Protection Strategies

Protection when downloading files

Be very careful when downloading files from a commercial Web site or a private BBS. McAfee's WebScan can scan files for infection before they enter your system. Alternatively, create a temporary download folder on your hard drive to store downloaded files. Use VirusScan to scan any files before you open them. If a file does contain a virus, it won't be started until the file is opened or executed. Therefore, you can remove it from your system without infecting other areas of your system. Also, be aware of the server's reputation. Corporate servers often have more incentives to keep their files clean compared to small private bulletin boards or newsgroups.

Scanning your portable media only takes minutes (usually not even that long). It's one of the best habits you can develop for your computer. These simple steps are easily worthwhile. This is especially true when you consider the alternative is possibly catching a virus and taking time to restore your data and programs from backups (assuming you made backups).

Additional suggestions

We've mentioned the importance of being careful about what goes into your system. The following are steps you can take that to prevent additional infection and limit damage from a virus that does infect your system.

❖ Use an antivirus program that can detect viruses before they integrate with your system.

❖ Establish and follow a routine of frequent backups. If catastrophe should strike, then you will have clean copies of your programs to reload. You'll realize the time spent backing up was a wise investment if your system becomes infected. This is especially true when you consider the potential damage from a particularly virulent or malicious virus.

❖ Arm yourself with information, updates and alerts. McAfee virus protection software includes a subscription to receive updates and vaccines for the latest viruses. The World Wide Web also has several sites that contain recent virus alerts. Many of these sites include background and supplementary information. The Anti-Virus Center (www.antivirus.com) and the National Computer Security Association (www.ncsa.com) are two popular and reliable sites for obtaining the latest virus news.

❖ Save shared data files or E-mail attachments in ASCII or RTF formats. Because neither format saves macros or formatting information, they'll act as a screen for filtering out macro viruses. This isn't practical if you need to work with the formatting data. However, if you're just reading the text, this step greatly increases your security against viruses.

If you're uncertain a file is "clean," scan the file before using it from your PC. If the file in question is a program file, don't run it. If it's a text file, don't load it. Regardless of how you got the file, scan it. There have even been cases where new blank, formatted diskettes were virus-infected.

Protection against boot sector viruses

Boot sector viruses make up 75% of all computer viruses. Follow these steps to protect yourself from these viruses:

Always use a password to boot up your computer:

❖ Click the [Start] and select the **Settings/Control Panel** command. Double-click on the Passwords icon to open the Passwords Property Sheet. If it isn't on top, click the "Change Password" tab.

❖ Click the [Change Windows Password...] button. Now enter the old password, if any and the new password. Then enter the new password again to confirm it.

Protection Strategies

❖ Click [OK] and your new password is set. This denies access to everyone except those with the keyword.

❖ Before typing in the password to boot up your computer, make certain you have no infected diskettes in any of your drives.

❖ After writing to a diskette and scanning it for viruses, make certain to write-protect it. Do this by sliding the tab in the upper corner of the diskette so the window is open. When a diskette is write-protected, the drive cannot write any data onto the diskette (including viruses).

❖ Use a secure password for your screen saver.

❖ Use an anti-virus program with a high rate of virus detection. Make certain it's properly installed on your system.

❖ Remember to keep your virus software's data files up to date.

❖ Boot sector/partition table viruses account for about 75% of all virus infections. Among the various boot sector/partition table viruses are Stoned and Michelangelo. These viruses are common and more difficult to track down because they don't change a file's size or affect its performance. These viruses are virtually invisible until their triggers are pulled.

Stoned, the most prevalent virus, is a common virus that will overwrite the master boot record of a hard diskette when the machine is booted from an infected diskette. From there it will infect other diskettes used on the machine, damaging files on those disks.

Michelangelo, the most infamous, has been known since April 1991. It was once very widespread. However, education and virus scanning software have severely limited its impact. Those that do become infected by Michelangelo will have their hard drives reformatted on March 6.

Protecting against program file viruses

The following steps will protect you from file infector computer viruses:

Change all your startup files, such as AUTOEXEC.BAT, CONFIG.SYS, WIN.INI, SYSTEM.INI, PROTOCOL.INI and MSMAIL.INI to read-only. This won't stop all viruses, but will halt most.

To do this, go to DOS and use the ATTRIB ("attribute") command. Then enter, for example:

```
ATTRIB +R C:\AUTOEXEC.BAT
```

This sets the AUTOEXEC.BAT file on the C: drive to read only. This will stop information from being written to the file. To turn off the read-only attribute, run the same command but replace "+R" with "-R":

```
ATTRIB -R C:\AUTOEXEC.BAT
```

You may repeat this with each system file. Using software to change a file's attributes is a good precaution, but isn't fail-safe. Anything that can be done by software can be undone by software—and a virus is a form of software.

Set the read-only attribute for program files, including the following extensions: .386, .BIN, .COM, .DLL, .DRV, .FON, .EXE, .OVL, .SYS and .VXD. Use the mouse to right-click on the program and select "Properties" from the pop-up menu. At the bottom of the General tab check the box next to "Read-only."

Setting the read-only attribute for Word

This will prevent some viruses from penetrating into the file, but not all. A sophisticated virus could remark these attributes to its own purposes.

If you believe you have a virus in RAM, switch off your PC. Then wait a minute before switching it on again. Don't use the reset button or press $\boxed{\text{Ctrl}}$ + $\boxed{\text{Alt}}$ + $\boxed{\text{Del}}$. A warm boot will not necessarily erase memory-resident viruses from the cache.

Use a secure password for your screen saver. Buy an anti-virus program with a high rate of virus detection. Make certain it's properly installed on your system. Remember to keep your virus program's data files up-to-date.

Protection against macro viruses

You can protect Microsoft Word from most macro viruses by turning off the autoexecute macro:

1. Select the **Macro...** command from the **Tools** menu.

2. Type "AUTOEXEC" where it says "Macro name:".

3. Click (Create) button.

4. Add the following commands to the macro:

```
Sub MAIN
DisableAutoMacros
MsgBox "AutoMacros are now turned off.", "Virus protection", 64
End Sub
```

5. Select **Save Template** in the **File** menu. When asked, "Do you want to keep changes to the macro Global: Autoexec?" click (Yes). This disables the tool used by most macro viruses, thus making those viruses impotent in your system. If you open an infected document, your system and other documents are safe. The infected document, however, remains infected. If opened in a version of Word that does not have the disabled autoexec described above, it will infect that copy of Word and any documents used with it. Colors, also called Rainbow, is the only known virus that is immune to this "vaccine."

When you start up Word, this macro runs automatically. It turns off the feature CONCEPT, DMV, NUCLEAR and other macro viruses use to infect Word documents. Since virus programmers will likely develop a method to overcome this with future macro viruses, we still recommend scanning for viruses with VirusScan or similar product.

6. Change the normal.dot template to read-only. To do this, select the **Tools/Options...** command in Word. In the Options dialog box, click on "File Locations" and identify the folder associated with User Templates.

Write down this path and directory if you need. Close the Options box, minimize Word and open the Templates folder. Right-click on "normal.dot" and click "Properties" in the pop-up menu. Check the box next to "Read-only".

Set the read-only attribute for normal.dot to prevent macro viruses

This will prevent most viruses from writing to your template and thus prevent their infecting additional documents.

MS-Word is used around the world. It includes editions that are tailored to different language groups. Some commands that are used in Word are the same in every version. However, other commands have been translated into their particular language edition. If a macro-virus uses a command from one version that isn't available on another version, the virus cannot infect the second system. For example, a virus that uses a German language macro command cannot infect English versions of Word.

For all types of viruses, if you haven't used a file, program or diskette before, scan it before you use it. Most viruses are passed accidentally, without the user realizing that the diskette he or she passed to you has a virus. Trusting a person doesn't mean you have to trust their software. This is true for friends, coworkers and even software companies. If it's new to you, scan it before using it.

The steps you will take to protect your computer from viruses depend on how you use your computer and how you exchange files with others. Scan everything if you're in an extremely high-risk environment. Do it several times a day, if necessary.

This maybe overkill for most private users. If you rarely exchange data or files with anyone else or another computer, your risk is much smaller but not zero. Consider your use patterns and build your virus protection strategy around that. Virus protection software is an important element in maintaining a safe, clean system.

The most important element is user education. Make certain each user of your computer knows how to use the scanning software. They should also recognize some of the symptoms of an infection. Also, everyone should know what to do when an infection is discovered. This could simply be notifying the primary user and waiting for help.

Removing viruses

All the vitamin C in the world won't make you 100% immune to all biological viruses. Similarly, no amount of precautions will make your computer system 100% safe from a computer virus. After all, sneaking through detection is the main goal of virus creators; the payload is moot if the virus can't get into your system. If you do get a virus on board, you'll want to remove it quickly to limit the spread of the infection.

❖ Keep your wits about you!

❖ Turn off your PC and reboot it from a clean, write-protected startup diskette.

❖ Run your virus detection software to locate and fix the contaminated files. If the damage is so extensive that your antivirus software cannot repair it, replace the infected files with clean backup copies (assuming you made backup copies)..

❖ To be on the safe side, run the virus detection software one more time. In most cases the virus will be gone and your system will be back to normal.

❖ If your virus detection software runs into something it cannot handle, call tech support right away.

There is no guarantee that your efforts to remove the virus will "cover all the bases." There is a good chance that you'll miss files if you manually attempt to remove the virus. Keep in mind, infected documents can be on diskettes, tapes, in E-mail attachments, etc. Multipartite viruses are particularly tricky to remove because of their wide infection zone. Use the antivirus program's clean or delete functions to root out all manifestations of a virus on your computer.

Scan, clean and back up local machines on a regular basis. You can do this manually or configure a schedule for automatic scans. Win 95 users will need the Microsoft PlusPack scheduling agent to schedule regular virus scans.

Teach all users of the computer about viruses. For example, a dialog box with the number "1" in Word indicates the loaded document is infected with a virus (the Concept macro). Give the user a person to contact or tell him/her what to do.

CREATING AN EMERGENCY STARTUP DISK

DOS and Windows users need to have a clean startup diskette to boot their systems in case of an irrecoverable virus infection.

Creating a startup diskette requires that your computer be free of viruses. Otherwise, viruses that are on your computer could be copied to your startup diskette and attack your system anew. If your computer has a virus, find a different computer running the same version of DOS as your computer. To check the version, go to the DOS prompt and enter "VER". Run antivirus software to ensure that this computer is free of viruses, and then do the following:

Go to the DOS prompt (C:\). In Windows 3.x choose the **File/Exit** command. In Win 95, click the MS-DOS prompt in the Start menu or "Restart in MS-DOS mode" from the Shut Down menu.

1. Insert a blank diskette into drive A: (remember, this procedure will overwrite any data on the diskette)

2. Now enter the following command at the C: prompt to format the diskette:

```
FORMAT A: /S/U
```

"Format A:" tells the computer to format the diskette in drive A:. The "S" switch instructs it to format it as a system diskette, copying IO.SYS, MSDOS.SYS and COMMAND.COM to the diskette (though IO.SYS and MSDOS.SYS are hidden files, so you won't see them if you run the DIR command on the diskette). "U" instructs the computer to perform an unconditional format, wiping the diskette clean. If you have a version of DOS earlier than 5.0, don't use the "U" switch, as an unconditional format is the default procedure. If you need to find out what version DOS you are running, type "VER" at the DOS prompt.

You will then be prompted to type in a volume label, with a maximum of 11 characters. Now you've got a clean (virus free) startup diskette. When you have VirusScan installed on your computer, follow these steps to make things easier:

3. Insert your virus free startup diskette into drive A:

4. Type the following command at the C: prompt to find SCAN.EXE: DIR SCAN.EXE /S.

5. Write down the path to this file. If you find multiple versions of SCAN.EXE, be sure to use the latest version.

6. Now change to the directory containing the latest version. To do this, type the CD command, followed by the path to SCAN.EXE. For example, you might type: CD \McAfee\Viruscan.

7. As soon as you are in the correct directory, copy the following files to your startup diskette:

```
COPY SCAN.EXE A: (press ENTER)
COPY SCAN.DAT A: (press ENTER)
COPY CLEAN.DAT A: (press ENTER)
COPY NAMES.DAT A: (press ENTER)
```

8. Now go back to the root directory (type CD\ and press ENTER)

9. Copy DOS programs to your startup diskette also:

```
COPY C:\WINDOWS\COMMAND\CHKDSK.* A: (press ENTER)
```

If you are running DOS 6.2 or later copy SCANDISK instead of CHKDSK. These utilities look for and repair errors on a diskette, hard or diskette.

```
COPY C:\WINDOWS\COMMAND\MEM.* A: (press ENTER)
```

This command will enable you to see how much memory is available on your system, and where it is allocated.

```
COPY C:\WINDOWS\COMMAND\DEBUG.* A: (press ENTER)
```

DEBUG is a program testing and editing tool. You'll probably never have to use it, but it provides a host of features to your system.

```
COPY C:\WINDOWS\COMMAND\DISKCOPY.* A: (press ENTER)
```

DISKCOPY will copy an entire diskette onto another diskette.

```
COPY C:\WINDOWS\COMMAND\FDISK.* A: (press ENTER)
```

FDISK allows you to partition your hard drive into several virtual hard drives for use with DOS.

```
COPY C:\WINDOWS\COMMAND\FORMAT.* A: (press ENTER)
```

FORMAT is the command to format a diskette so it can be read by your computer. Formatting a diskette deletes all the information on that diskette.

```
COPY C:\WINDOWS\COMMAND\LABEL.* A: (press ENTER)
```

You can assign individual names to diskettes and drives with the LABEL command.

```
COPY C:\WINDOWS\COMMAND\UNDELETE.* A: (press ENTER)
```

UNDELETE will help you recover data that is accidentally erased.

```
COPY C:\WINDOWS\COMMAND\SYS.* A: (press ENTER)
```

The SYS command will copy the DOS system files to a diskette of your designation.

```
COPY C:\WINDOWS\COMMAND\XCOPY.* A: (press ENTER)
```

While the COPY command copies individual files, XCOPY will copy entire directories for you.

If you run a diskette compression utility, you also need to copy the drivers for accessing the compressed drive to your startup diskette.

NOTE

Make certain to label and write-protect your startup diskette. When you write protect it, you are preventing viruses from infecting the diskette. Then store it in a safe place. These are all files and/or commands that your system will need if the worst-case scenario is enacted on your hard drive. You can learn more about these items in your system manual. The library and Internet are two more good resources for information on DOS commands.

ANTIVIRUS PROGRAMS AND SOFTWARE

As viruses have developed, so have antivirus programs. They now use several strategies to combat the many viruses. Antivirus programs scan for the byte pattern, or *signature*, that most viruses copy from file to file as they replicate. Powerful antivirus programs can even detect small pieces of unique repeating code to catch polymorphous viruses. Components of antivirus programs called *integrity checkers* or *checksummers* monitor files. When they notice an unexpected increase in size or other strange behavior, these programs will notify you of potential infection.

37

Behavior blockers will prevent suspicious activity before damage can be done. For example, if a program tells the computer to overwrite the master boot record, a blocker program will intercept the order and notify you of the suspicious command.

Virus detectors adapted for the Internet can monitor browser files and E-mail attachments to insure clean downloads. Some can check zipped and self-extracting files for viruses before you open them on your system.

Most antivirus programs will incorporate all these strategies in their virus hunts and most have similar capabilities. When choosing an antivirus program, make sure that it performs the following three important tasks:

❖ Detection

❖ Prevention

❖ Removal

You should also make certain it covers all of your media:

❖ Hard drives

❖ Floppy drives

❖ Network drives

❖ CD-ROM drives

The antivirus program should also operate in the background without interfering in your work. It should be updated frequently to stay current with new viruses.

VirusScan

McAfee is the industry leader for protection against viruses. Their flagship program is called VirusScan. It is used by millions of corporate and individual users in over 65 countries. VirusScan consistently detects over 96% of the more than 6500 known viruses.

Its patented technology efficiently pinpoints known, generic and even new and unknown viruses of all types and variations. VirusScan receives monthly certifications from NCSA (National Computer Security Association) and VSUM (Virus Information Summary List), two authoritative virus databases. These ensure that McAfee is up-to-date on the latest or most important viruses by submitting hundreds of samples for study each month.

VirusScan effectively and efficiently protects your drives from intrusive viruses. It will also keep a log of the viral activity and responses to it. This can be very helpful if you need to backtrack an infection.

VirusScan uses three programs to continually monitor and protect your system.

❖ VShield
Looks for viruses whenever you turn on or reset your computer, launch a program, copy files or access a diskette.

❖ Scan
Detects and removes viruses during programmed searches. Scanning profiles can be automated to suit your needs.

❖ Validate
Authorizes VirusScan updates as genuine and unaltered.

You may configure VirusScan to notify you when a virus is found and await your command or to automatically clean or delete the file. The recursive scanning identifies and repairs most infections to their original state, even complicated multiple reinfections.

VirusScan's 32-bit scanning engine quickly checks for viruses in all programs, master boot record, boot sectors, system files and VirusScan's own files. You can set it up to check your entire system, including local and network drives, CD-ROMs, diskettes, file allocations and partition tables, folders, files and compressed files.

If it detects any viruses, VirusScan will prevent infected programs from launching (thereby preventing spread of the virus) and refuse warm boots from an infected diskette. VirusScan cannot, however, prevent you from starting (cold booting) from an infected diskette. This is how 80% of infections are passed; boot from your hard drive by making certain the diskette drives are empty before starting your system.

3 Protection Strategies

WebScan

WebScan protects you when browsing the Internet or receiving E-mail attachments. It keeps viruses off your system by checking executable and MS-Word files before they get into your system, even zip-compressed and self-extracting files. If a file you desire is infected, WebScan will alert you. From there you may discontinue the download or download it into a temporary directory for immediate cleaning with VirusScan.

WebScan and VirusScan are designed to work together. WebScan protects your system from viruses traveling the Web and Internet. VirusScan cleans out any viruses that sneak aboard.

McAfee is the industry leader because VirusScan and WebScan are strong, efficient products that have proven themselves through time. People have learned to trust V-Scan and W-Scan to provide exactly what they promise plus strong after-purchase support of updates and service.

There is a lot you can do to protect your computer and its data from viruses. McAfee's antivirus software will prevent, detect and remove computer viruses. The system itself can be configured to be less vulnerable to viruses. Most importantly, the users of your computer(s) can learn about viruses and how to keep them off your system.

McAfee's VirusScan

Chapter 4

What's In This Chapter

McAfee's VirusScan

McAfee is the undisputed leader in virus prevention, detection and disinfection. Founded by John McAfee in 1989, McAfee established its presence by marketing its early products as shareware, allowing users to try the programs out before purchasing.

McAfee was one of the first companies to achieve real success through shareware distribution, a circulation scheme now used by many software vendors. Electronic distribution and a quality product spread McAfee to millions of individual and corporate users in over sixty-five countries around the world.

McAfee is well-known and most used because their products perform better than any other virus protection scheme and because of their excellent after-purchase support. VirusScan has a 20% better detection rate of viruses than the number two market contender and consistently detects more than an amazing 96% of the more than five thousand known viruses.

Furthermore, their scanning technique can even detect unknown viruses, even viruses that haven't been written yet, by looking for generic virus characteristics and actions. The 32-bit scanning engine in VirusScan for Windows 95 uses virtual device drivers (VxD technology) to automatically detect any memory-resident viruses.

The on-access scanning features look for viruses every time you access a new disk or run a new program, and covers all of your system areas. Multiple reinfections can be particularly difficult to repair, but VirusScan's recursive scanning can even detect and repair these otherwise corrupted files.

VirusScan can be purchased from retail stores or from McAfee's Web site where you can download the program.

INSTALLING VIRUSSCAN

Before installing VirusScan, disable any other virus protection running on your computer and shut down open applications. VirusScan will scan your system for viruses, install VirusScan, make necessary changes to your startup files and activate VirusShield during the installation. If you are installing the program from floppy disks, use Windows's **Start/Run...** menu to execute A:\setup.exe (where "A:" is your floppy drive). This begins the install wizard.

If installing from a downloaded zip file, unpack the file and run SETUP.EXE.

Click the Next> button. Select "Express" to install VirusScan for optimal security on your system.

Select "Custom" to install components of VirusScan.

By default, VirusScan will be installed into C:\Program Files\McAfee.

If you would like to place it elsewhere, click [Browse...] and select your directory of choice.

Click the [Next>] button and select where you would like program icons to be installed.

Click the [Next>] button.

VirusScan will be installed to your system. It will modify your AUTOEXEC.BAT file to launch VirusShield when your computer starts.

Click [OK] to scan your system.

If no viruses were found, click [OK] again. The "whatsnew.doc" file has information for new users and technical specifications.

After installation is complete you need to restart the computer for virus protection to be activated.

If a virus is detected during installation, restart from a clean, write-protected system disk. You may use either a disk that came with your system (like the Win 95 Emergency Recovery Diskette) or a backup that you've made. Read Chapter 3 for instructions on how to create an emergency backup diskette.

After you've booted the system from this clean disk, remove the startup disk and insert the McAfee Emergency Disk. Go to the DOS prompt and enter:

```
SCAN /ADL /CLEAN /ALL
```

to search all files on all drives (excepting floppy diskettes). The Scan program on the Emergency Disk will locate and clean any viruses in your system.

Now remove the diskette, restart your PC normally and continue with installation. If Scan found a virus that could not be removed, note the name of the corrupted file so that you can restore it from uninfected backups and enter:

```
SCAN /CLEAN /DEL
```

to remove the corrupted file and the virus responsible from your system. Now restart the computer and begin installation again. After VirusScan is installed, replace the file that was damaged from a clean backup copy.

Most viruses are transmitted through floppy diskettes. Therefore, after you've installed VirusScan you should scan and disinfect all your floppy disks to be sure that none of them are virus carriers.

To scan diskettes, right click on the Start button and click "Scan for Viruses" on the menu that appears. This will display the main VirusScan window. Choose the "Reports" tab to configure how VirusScan informs you of its progress.

McAfee's VirusScan

Information you enter on the "Where and What" tab tells VirusScan where to look and what types of files to scan.

To scan diskettes enter "A:" in the "Scan in:" field on the "Where and What" page, insert a diskette in the drive and click "Scan Now." Infected files, if any are found, will be displayed and dealt with as you directed on the Actions tab.

To scan diskettes enter "A:" in the "Scan in:" field on the "Where and What" page, insert a diskette in the drive and click "Scan Now." Infected files, if any are found, will be displayed and dealt with as you directed on the Actions tab.

FEATURES OF VIRUSSCAN

VirusScan is actually three programs:

❖ VirusScan
performs on-demand scanning for all types of viruses

❖ VirusShield
operates in the background, scanning programs and disks as you call for them

❖ Validate
used to make certain that the VirusScan program files and database updates are unaltered.

Joined with user education, the most essential aspect of any virus protection scheme, these programs will create and maintain a virus-free environment on your computer.

The only ways VirusScan can be compromised are through:

❖ Carelessness

❖ If you neglect updates over time newer viruses may elude detection

❖ If you boot the computer with an infected diskette in a drive, the virus will boot into the computer before virus protection can be enabled.

Always make certain the disk drives are empty before starting your system. If an infected floppy is booted, the virus will be passed to your computer, even if the boot isn't successful. If you don't boot from unknown floppies, do keep your virus database up to date, and scan new downloaded files before executing them, you should be able to maintain a virus-free computing environment.

VirusShield

VirusShield provides on-access scanning across your system. It uses virtual device drivers in Windows 95 to scan independently of DOS. On a Windows 3.x system, VirusShield acts as a DOS TSR (terminate and stay resident in memory) program. Both intercept and scan programs as they execute. VirusShield checks programs, the master boot record, boot sectors, system files and the VirusScan program files themselves for virus signatures. It will prevent infected programs from running and will prevent warm boots (pressing Reset or Ctrl + Alt + Del) from an infected disk. Again, no component of VirusScan can prevent you from cold booting from an infected disk.

USING VIRUSSCAN

Using VirusScan with Windows 95

If you have Windows 95 running on your system, Scan95 is the scanning and cleansing component of VirusScan. Windows 3.x machines use WScan for these operations. Scan95 and WScan have essentially the same features, but with interfaces that have been designed for their specific operating environment.

You have several ways to start VirusScan under Windows 95:

1. Click the Start button and choose **Programs/McAfee VirusScan95/VirusScan95** from the Start menu

2. Right-click on the Start button and choose "Scan for Viruses" from the pop-up menu.

3. Use Windows Explorer (or another shell) to locate the McAfee\VirusScan folder and double-click the Scan95 program.

4. Create a shortcut and place it on the desktop. To create a shortcut, use Explorer to go to the Scan95 program, right-click the file and drag it to your desktop. When you release the button, choose Create Shortcut Here. Now you can double-click the shortcut link to execute the program.

5. Right-click on any drive, folder or executable file (including .DOC files) and choose "Scan for Viruses" from the pop-up display.

Scan95 interface

The Scan95 interface is pretty self-explanatory to those users familiar with Windows's conventions. I'll run through it here with you for those new users, and those who want to know all the details about the programs they are using.

The file menu has three commands: **Save Settings**, **View Activity Log** and **Close**.

McAfee's VirusScan

Select **Close** to exit the program. The Activity Log will help you keep track of what was scanned and the results of those scans. If you do find a virus, this log may help you identify when and how the virus entered your system, and if necessary, help you recover data. Setting up a log will be explained in a moment.

The **Save Settings** command lets you record the entered scanning profile as the new default settings or as a scan profile. You may want to set a profile for scanning diskettes, and another for scanning hard drives, for instance. This will save you from having to enter the same settings each time you want to scan a particular component of your system.

The **Help** menu provides on-line assistance.

Selecting **About** will get you information on the specific version of Scan95 that you are using. If you have questions about the interface, choose **What's This?** from the **Help** menu and your cursor will include a question mark. Now click on the object you want to know more about to receive a brief description.

For more detailed explanations, choose **Help Topics** from the **Help** menu. You can use the Contents, Index or Find pages to locate information by subject. McAfee did a good job loading this Help feature with information explaining the features and functions of Scan95. Since it is easily accessed directly through Scan95's interface, this should be your first stop when you have a question.

Use the tabbed pages to configure the scan settings. The "Where and What" page sets the parameters for the scan.

Entering a drive or path in the "Scan in:" field tells Scan95 what area of your system you want checked for viruses. Check the box next to "Include subfolders" to scan the entire contents of a directory. Clear this box to scan just files within the directory you specify, but not inside the folders within that directory.

The lower portion of the Where and What page is where you'll tell Scan95 what files you want scanned. Selecting "All Files" will scan all of the files in the directory specified above.

Highlighting the box next to "Compressed Files" will have Scan95 look inside compressed LZEXE and PKLITE files. If you select "Program Files Only" you should click the [Program Files...] button to make sure that the program files you want are indicated here.

Use the [Add...] and [Delete] buttons to edit the file types to be scanned as program files. The default selection is the most complete scan of program files, but you can speed up the scan time by choosing to scan only the file types with which you regularly work. If you import and export a lot of Word documents but don't work with files that affect your drivers, for instance, you could enter .DOT and .DOC and remove the extensions for .DRV and .VXD. This will set the scan to catch macros in Word files and save time by skipping driver files.

The "Actions" tab instructs Scan95 what to do when it encounters a virus. Scan95 can continue scanning, prompt you for an action, clean the infection or delete the infected file(s). Highlighting one of these will bring you a brief description in the Scan95 window.

When you select "Continue Scanning," Scan95 will scan through the target and deliver any viruses found at the end of the scan. Selecting "Prompt for Action" will cause Scan95 to stop after each virus is discovered and ask you what you want to do with it.

"Clean Infected File" will automatically attempt to clean any infection it encounters, and "Delete Infected File" will do just that. This last option is the safest way to contain and expunge viruses, but you are also going to lose those files that are infected. This is a fine choice when you have backups of all your files, but be sure that you have complete backups.

"Continue Scanning" is my preferred selection because it allows me to deal with viruses as a group. I'm not involved in detailed virus analysis, so it isn't necessary for me to work with them individually. I just want to keep my system safe and clean, while monitoring what's going on inside my system at the same time.

The "Reports" tab is where you configure the response Scan95 will make to you after a scan.

If you selected "Prompt user for action" on the Actions page, you can mark the box next to "Display message" and enter your message in the space provided. When a virus is encountered this message will be displayed to the user. You may want to instruct the user who to contact or what action he or she should take. This message is only displayed when Scan95 prompts the user to take an action.

Highlighting "Sound Alert" causes Scan95 to beep when it discovers a virus, thus drawing attention to the computer's illness. Mark "Log to File" to keep a record of scans and infections. Enter the path and file to record this log or navigate to it with the Browse... button. You can limit the size of the log with the check box and size parameter on the bottom of the page.

Press the [Scan Now] button when you are ready to let Scan95 search through the specified files. "Stop" will interrupt a scan in progress. Pressing "New Scan" will reset each of the pages to their default parameters so you can configure a new scan. If you will want to reuse the scan parameters you have entered, go to the file menu and select "Save Settings."

Features of VirusScan with Windows 3.x

Seven buttons are available when you open the WScan program window:

- ❖ [Profiles]   ❖ [Scan]   ❖ [Select]
- ❖ [Settings]   ❖ [Virus List] ❖ [Schedule]   ❖ [Activity Log]

These commands and dialog boxes are also available through the menu bar. Use the profiles button to run a preconfigured scan profile. (Setting a scan profile in Windows 3.x requires one to edit the WSCAN.INI file. Consult your Windows manual or McAfee's on-line help and manual for more information on configuring a scan profile.)

Click the [Scan] button to run a scan with the current settings.

The" Select" page, available through the button or **File** menu, is where you select the drive(s), directory and/or file(s) to scan.

Your selections are listed in the window on the right. Use the [Add...] and [Remove] buttons to edit your selections. You can select your hard drive(s) from the Drives pull-down menu. Selecting a drive in this way scans all the files in all the directories on that drive. Selecting a directory from the directory list will scan all the files in that directory, but not files in subdirectories. Each directory must be selected individually from the directory list.

Clicking [Settings] will open the settings notebook, with a page each for "Controls", "Action", "Reports", "Validation" and "Exceptions".

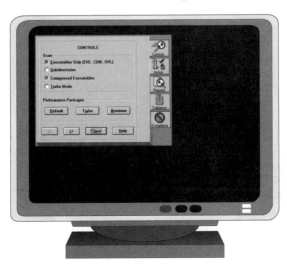

Choose what file types to scan on the "Controls" page. You can also select a "performance package" here. The "Turbo" option is a faster, less comprehensive scan. It scans just as many files, but looks at a smaller portion of each file, and so may miss a stealthy virus. The "Maximum" mode checks all subdirectories, files and files compressed with LZEXE or PKLITE. It takes longer but is much more thorough.

The "Action" page determines the automatic action to be taken by VirusScan when a virus is found. You may configure WScan to clean, delete or move infected files. Leaving these fields blank will notify you of the virus and let you act upon it then.

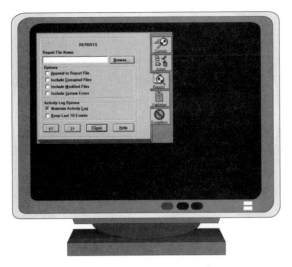

The Reports page lets you set up a report and log to record the scanning activity.

Validation checking stores file information (size, type, etc.) in a code appended to each file or in a separate file. It can then monitor your files for the type of unexpected change caused by viruses, and use the codes to restore the file to its original form. The boot sector and master boot record can not be validated with appended codes. To validate the system areas, store the codes in an external file, which is McAfee's recommended method. See "Validation" later in this chapter for a more complete discussion.

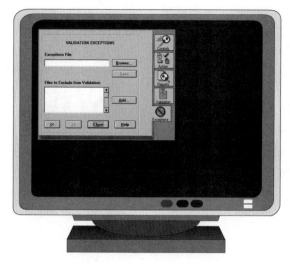

The "Exceptions" page is where you enter files which you don't want to be validated. Some programs contain a self-modifying code, and thusly will return a false alarm when validated. A few computers also self-modify their boot sector, and these also will return virus alarms though no virus is present. Enter these programs and disks on the exceptions page. You may enter them directly in the text field or use the Browse... button to locate any files you wish to exclude.

The [Virus List] button displays known viruses, the areas they can infect, their characteristics and whether the current version of VirusScan can clean the infection.

Use the [Schedule] button to configure an automatic scan. For a new scheduled scan, click [Add]. In the box to the lower left select the frequency of the scan (daily, weekly or monthly), the time the scan will occur and what items you want scanned. Pressing [Select] will open a window similar to the Select button window and Options will open a window similar to the Settings window.

Clicking the [Activity Log] button will bring you a summary of the scan activity.

Removing a virus

McAfee's VirusScan can find viruses in your computer. It can also help you remove them before they spread to other programs. Scan95 (for Win 95 users) and WScan (for Win 3.x users) can clean most infections, but if VirusScan finds a memory-resident virus or the master boot record or boot sector are infected, the most effective cleansing can be done with the DOS Scan program, which will be explained in a moment. If you are sure that no operating system or VirusScan files are infected and no viruses are resident in memory, you can use Scan95/WScan to safely clean your system.

Look in the subdirectory containing the VirusScan program files. For VirusScan to clean your system you must have the CLEAN.DAT file. If you don't have this file, it is available from McAfee's Bulletin Board (408-988-4004) or their Customer care phoneline (408-988-3832) can direct you to other sources.

Scan95

If you have "Clean infected file" or "Delete infected file" predefined in VirusScan's settings, Scan95 will respond automatically and notify you of the infections and actions taken. To remove viruses manually, choose "Continue Scanning" or "Prompt for Action" on VirusScan's Actions property page.

If you choose the latter, Scan95 will offer you four choices when it detects a virus. To continue scanning until all designated files are searched for viruses, choose "Continue". Select "Stop" to end the scan session. "Clean" will repair the infected file. "Delete" will remove and overwrite the infected file.

While scanning the designated files and drives, the names of the files being scanned are displayed in the status bar and any messages will appear in the main VirusScan window. When cleaning viruses, Scan95 will attempt to repair the boot sector and any infected files. It can repair the damage caused by most viruses, but some files can be damaged beyond repair.

If Scan95 can not safely repair a file, it will tell you the name of the file so you can restore it from a clean backup. Delete the infected file, run Scan95 again and when your system is clean, restore the corrupted files from virus-free backups.

WScan

In Windows 3.x, go to the "Actions" tab of the notebook or select **Settings/Actions** from the menu.

Here you may choose "Clean Infection", which will try to repair any infected files it finds; "Delete Infected File", which will delete infected files when it finds them; or "Move Infected File to Directory", which will copy the infected file to your quarantine directory and delete the original.

Highlight the "Clean Infection" box and click OK. Click the Scan icon or choose **Scan/Start Scan** from the menu. WScan will search the drives, directories and files you selected, with the file names being displayed in the status bar. When WScan pinpoints a virus it will attempt to restore the boot sector and any infected files. Most infections can be cleaned with WScan, but if a file is damaged beyond repair, WScan will tell you so and give you the file name(s) so you can restore from a clean backup. Delete the corrupted file(s), run WScan again and when the computer is virus-free, restore the damaged files.

If you have a master boot record, boot sector or memory-resident virus, do not use Scan95 or WScan to clean out the virus(es). Instead you should use the DOS Scan program after rebooting from a clean, write-protected system disk. See Chapter Three if you want to know how to create your own clean startup disk.

USING WITH DOS

SCAN

SCAN is the DOS component of VirusScan. Through command line options, Scan performs the same functions as Scan95 and WScan. It can also be used to remove troublesome virus types from a Windows-based machine.

In order to use Scan, the CLEAN.DAT file must be present in the subdirectory containing the VirusScan program files. If you don't have this file, contact McAfee, or download it from their BBS: 408-988-4004.

Navigate to a DOS prompt. If you are using Win 3.x, choose "Exit" from the file menu. In Win 95, click the MS-DOS prompt in the Start menu or select "Restart in MS-DOS mode" in the Shut Down menu.

If the virus was found in memory, shut down the computer and reboot from your clean, write-protected startup diskette. Go to the directory where VirusScan was installed (the default is C:\MCAFEE\VIRUSSCAN).

Enter the following:

```
SCAN /ADL /ALL /CLEAN
```

to exorcise any viruses and repair infected files.

Switch	Details
SCAN	Runs the program that will clean your system.
/ADL	Tells the program to scan all local drives, including hard drives, compressed drives and CD-ROM drives (but not floppy diskettes).
/ALL	Orders Scan to check all files for infections, not just the most likely victims.
/Clean	Repairs damaged files. Most files can be safely used again after cleaning.

If the virus(es) was safely removed and infected files are repaired, Scan will notify you of its success. If a file was corrupted beyond Scan's repair abilities, you will see the message "Virus cannot be removed from this file." Make note of the file name and then prepare to delete it. Run Scan again, but use the /DEL switch instead of the /CLEAN. Do not use DOS commands (DEL, for example) to remove viruses or virus-infected files. Doing so may result in loss of data and the inability to use the infected disk. You can restore the removed file(s) from a backup.

When Scan has removed the virus and repaired (or removed) infected files, restart your computer normally and rescan your system.

After finding a virus on your system, try to find out where it came from. If a diskette is the most likely culprit, scan your diskettes to prevent a reinfection. If you've been using floppies to transfer files you should also scan them. Even if they are not the source of the virus, they may have been infected while the virus was in your system, and if so they could reinfect it.

VALIDATION

Windows 3.x and DOS versions of VirusScan provide checksummer validation routines to look for virus activity. Validation checking records information about files (size, type, time/day stamp, etc.) and compares this to earlier checks. If suspicious activity is detected VirusScan will notify you. Through this detection method, VirusScan is able to detect viruses that haven't even been written yet. The recovery option will restore files that have been damaged by these viruses.

To set up a validation scan in Windows, go to the Settings notebook and select the "Validation" tab or click **Validation** in the **Settings** menu. The validation scan uses a code to save information about each file it scans.

Select "Use Codes Appended to Files" to append the validation codes to the executable and Word files themselves. This will validate files on a hard disk or floppy diskette, but not the master boot record or boot sector. This will add about 98 bytes to each file validated.

If you choose "Use Codes in External File," the validation codes are store in a file of your specification. Highlight the box next to this item and enter your desired file name in the field at right or choose Browse... to select one from the list that appears. This file will grow about 95 bytes for each file validated. This method will analyze files on hard disk, floppy diskette and system areas (the master boot record and boot sector). McAfee recommends using this option to store your validation codes.

Checking the "Add Codes" option will add the validation codes to the place you chose during the next scan.

Highlighting "Check Codes" will have WScan check the validation codes during your next scan.

"Remove Codes" will delete the validation information. When you add new software to your system you will have to update the validation codes. Do this by removing the validation codes, and then scan your system with "Add Codes" selected.

Some programs are self-modifying or perform self-checks. These files can trigger false alarms with validation virus detection. The Exceptions page in the Settings notebook lets you exclude these files from validation checking, thus avoiding false alarms. Many of the programs that operate this way will advise you to turn virus protection off before running them. Listing them on the exceptions page lets you keep VirusScan running with these programs without conflicts or false virus alarms.

The Exceptions File contains the list of files to exclude from validation. Type the path and file name in the text box or browse existing files by clicking the Add button.

The list of excluded files can be seen in "Files to Exclude from Validation." To add a new file, enter its path and name in the entry field or click "Add" and select it from the list. To remove an entry from the list, highlight it by clicking on it and then press the Del key on your keyboard.

Validation codes in DOS work the same way, but obviously have a different interface. In DOS you still have two ways to store validation codes.

Using the "F" option will store the codes in a separate file. This is a slower scanning method but will not modify the files themselves and can be used to detect changes to the master boot record and boot sector of your disks. This is the McAfee recommended method.

The "V" options append the validation codes to the files checked. This is a noticeably quicker option, but self-modifying files may report false alarms. This also won't check the system areas for changes.

> **NOTE**
>
> Some PCs, notably older Hewlett-Packard and Zenith machines, modify the boot sector each time they are booted. In your computer's documentation, check to see if your PC employs self-modifying boot code. If it does, using validation codes stored in a separate file will invariably bring up a false alarm reporting that your boot sector has been modified. The report is true, except there is no virus present. If your PC operates this way, use the "V" option or record the boot sector in your list of exceptions.

To record validation codes to their own file, navigate to the directory containing the VirusScan program (default=C:\MCAFEE\VIRUSSCAN) and enter "SCAN /ADL /AF C:\VALCODES.VSC." This will scan all the local drives for viruses, create validation codes for the files scanned and record those codes in a file (valcodes.vsc) in the root of C:.

Once you have established the codes you can use them to scan for unauthorized file changes by getting to the directory in which VirusScan was installed and scanning the local drives by entering "SCAN /ADL /CF C:\VALCODES.VSC."

If Scan reports any infections, you can clean them by performing another scan with the addition of the "\CLEAN" switch. This will use the recovery codes to repair infected files.

After installing new software you will need to update the validation and recovery codes by deleting them and creating new ones. You may do this with the DOS command (DEL C:\VALCODES.VSC) or through VirusScan:

Enter the following from the directory to which VirusScan was installed:

```
SCAN /ADL /RF C:\VALCODES.VSC
```

to delete the codes and scan again with the "/AF" switch to create new codes.

DOS Scan Options	
Switch	Details
/AF	Adds validation and recovery codes to a separate file.
/CF	Checks files by comparing validation codes and current status of files.
/RF	Removes validation codes
/AV	Appends validation and recovery codes to the executable and MS-Word files.
/CV	Checks files by comparing appended validation codes to the current status of the files.
/RV	Removes appended validation codes.

To use appended validation codes, follow the procedure described above, replacing the "F" switch with the appropriate "V" switch and omitting the target C:\VALCODES.VSC.

KEEPING A LOG

Every adventurer and scientist keeps a log of discoveries and observations. This helps them to know where they've been, what's happened, and maybe what's about to happen. You should also keep a log as you track, observe, capture and kill viruses within your computer system. This will help you monitor the scanning activity and can enable you to pinpoint when and where a virus initially infected your system.

Terms you should know:

❖ Report
Reports the items scanned, infections found and cleaned, and details about corrupted files, modified files and system errors.

❖ Log
Tracks the date and time of scans, items scanned and infections found.

❖ Notification
An immediate warning to the user that a virus has been found.

SAVING SCAN RESULTS

Saving scan results with Scan95

Open the main VirusScan window by right clicking the Start menu and clicking "Scan for Viruses." Click the Reports tab to display the Reports property page.

Mark the box next to "Log to File" to keep a record of the virus activity. By default, information will be saved to a text file in C:\Program Files\McAfee. You may choose another location by entering a path and file name in the text field or using the Browse... button to select a file. You may also set a limit to the size of the log, anywhere from 10 to 999 KB.

Saving scan results with WScan

Open the "Reports" page of the settings notebook by selecting **Settings/Reports** from the menu bar or clicking the Settings button and choosing the "Reports" tab.

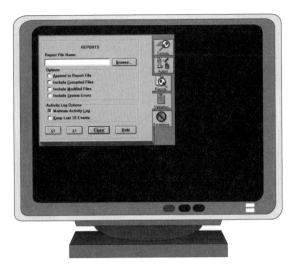

Enter the name of the file you want to create or update in the Report File Name field or use the [Browse...] button to seek one. The default file extension is .VSS. If you record a report to an existing file, you can instruct WScan to append the new information to the end of the extant file. If you don't select this option, the new report will overwrite the old one. Selecting "Include Corrupted Files" will save information about files damaged beyond repair in the report. Corrupted files must be isolated or removed to prevent spreading the infection. To record information on validated files that have been modified, mark the box next to "Include Modified Files."

Selecting "Include System Errors" will add information about problems that occur during the scan to the report. WScan will save the time/day stamp of the scan and its results when you configure it to "Maintain Activity Log." This log is SCAN.LOG in the current directory by default.

Keep Last x Events lets you retain log entries for the most recent scans, or the last hundred. You can change this value by adjusting the "KeepLogOnly" or "Last $x=0$" setting in the WSCAN.INI file, where "x" is the number of entries to save.

The online Help can help you get you more information on WSCAN.INI. To view the activity log, click its icon or click "Activity Log" in the **Scan** menu. For more details about a particular scan, highlight the entry and click [Details]. This will tell you what items were scanned and what viruses, if any, were found.

Use the (Print) button to get a hard copy of the log. You may also print, view or edit the log by opening the file (VSCAN.LOG by default) in a word processor or text editor. If you want to change the log's file name, this can be done in the WSCAN.INI file.

Saving scan results with SCAN

Go to the directory where VirusScan was installed.

Enter the following:

```
SCAN C: /REPORT C:\VIRUS.LOG
```

to scan the C: drive and create a report titled VIRUS.LOG on the C: drive.

Your report can be enhance with the following switches:

Switch	Details
/APPEND	New information will be appended at the end of the report file if the one you specified already exists. Otherwise, the new information will overwrite the old.
/LOG	Instructs Scan to record the time/date of a scan and its results by updating or creating an activity log.
/RPTALL	Lists all the files scanned in the report file.
/RPTCOR	Lists the names of non-executable files in the report. These may simply require another program to execute, or they be former executable files that have been damaged by a virus. Comparing /RPTCOR results with previous reports may show a file that was once an executable to be non-executable now, which can indicate virus corruption.
/RPTERR	Will record errors that occur during a scan.
/RPTMOD	If a validated file has been modified, information about it will be added to the report.

You can create an activity log for a brief record of your scans, tracking the time/date of scans, items scanned and infections found. From the directory where VirusScan is installed, enter:

```
SCAN C: /LOG
```

This will scan the C: drive and create a log in the default location (SCAN.LOG in the current directory). If this file already exists, Scan will update it with the new information. To view the log, enter:

```
SCAN /ADL /SHOWLOG /PAUSE
```

You can print, view and edit the activity log by opening it with a word processor or text editor.

To notify a user when a virus is encountered, create a short message in a text editor program that will be displayed when a virus is discovered. You may want to tell the user who to contact or what immediate steps to take when the computer encounters a virus. Save this message as a text file (.txt) in the VirusScan folder. Scan the local drives and activate notification by entering:

```
SCAN /ADL /CONTACTFILE C:\[PATH]\[ALERT.TXT]
```

where alert.txt is your message.

SCAN WALK-THROUGH

Windows 95

VirusScan integrates well with the Win 95 environment. Because of this there are a number of ways to conduct a virus scan. This example is just one route to ensuring a safe, clean system. It may be the easiest for you or you may find that another method works better for you and the configuration of your computer system. This walk through will introduce the main features of VirusScan for Windows 95. For more complete information, refer to the earlier part of this chapter, consult the McAfee manual if you already own VirusScan, McAfee's online help from the VirusScan menubar, or the wealth of information available from McAfee's Web site.

Step I

Right-click Windows's **Start** button

Step 2:

Click "Scan for Viruses" from the pop-up menu to open the main VirusScan window. If you have questions about anything you see in this window, select "What's this?" from the Help menu and click on the feature you want to know more about.

Step 3

On the "Where and What" tab, enter "C:" in the "scan in:" box. This is one of the broadest searches you will conduct. Searches may be narrowed to a single directory or file.

Step 4

Mark the following boxes
Include subfolders, Compressed files, and All files.

Step 5

Click the "Actions" tab and select "Prompt for action" from the pull-down menu. This will allow you to select the action to take for each infection found.

Step 6

Click the "Reports" tab and mark "Sound alert" and "Log to file." Make note of the default log location or enter another path of your preference.

Step 7

Click "Scan now." Because this is a large area to scan this will take a few minutes. You can watch the names of the directories being scanned scroll by at the bottom of the window and the number of files scanned just to the right of that.

Hopefully when the scan ends, the statement "No infected items were found" will be displayed at the bottom of the window. If any are found, they will be listed in the window and you will be prompted for action. Clean the infections and scan again to be sure you got them all. If the files are corrupted beyond repair, delete them and restore from clean backups.

WScan

Step 1

Double-click the WScan icon.

Step 2

Click the Settings button to open the notebook.

Step 3

On the Controls page, select "Subdirectories" and "Compressed Executables" by checking the box next to each item.

Step 4

Open the Reports page by clicking on its tab. Enter a file name for the report or use the Browse... button to select one. Check the boxes next to "Append to Report File," "Include Corrupted Files," "Include Modified Files," and "Include System Errors." At the bottom of the page highlight "Maintain Activity Log" and close the Settings window.

McAfee's VirusScan

Step 5

Click the Select button to choose the system areas you wish to scan. This time we are going to scan all the items on the C: drive. First, remove any items from the selections window on the right by highlighting it and clicking "Remove." Now highlight C: in the "Drives:"list and click the Add Drive button. Then click the OK button.

Step 5

Click the Select button to choose the system areas you wish to scan. This time we are going to scan all the items on the C: drive. First, remove any items from the selections window on the right by highlighting it and clicking "Remove." Now highlight C: in the "Drives:"list and click the Add Drive button. Then click the OK button.

Step 6

Click [Scan] to initiate the virus scan. The title bar will say "[scanning]" and the file names will appear at the bottom of the window as they are scanned. You can watch the progress in the Report frame and notices will appear in the "Messages:" frame. Because we are scanning all the files, not just executables, you will see messages that some of the files scanned "may not be executable." If you see this message when scanning executable files only, you may have damaged files, but this time many of the files being scanned were never meant to be executable.

When the scan finishes, you can see the results in the "Report" and "Messages:" frames. To view the report that you selected on the Reports page of the settings notebook, use Windows's file manager to locate the .VSS file that was created and highlight it. Now choose "Associate" from the **File** menu and link the .VSS extension to the Notepad program. After this, double-click on the .VSS file to view the report, which contains the same summary information that was reported when the scan finished, but you can keep this file for later reference.

DOS SCAN walkthrough

Step 1

Navigate to the directory in which you installed VirusScan.

Step 2

Enter the following:

```
SCAN C/ALL
```

This will scan all the files on your C: drive and may take a few minutes. If you have a quick eye you can monitor the file names as they are scanned.

VirusScan will notify you with a beep when it finishes. The summary information will tell you how many executable and MS-Word files were found (analyzed), the total number of files scanned and how many are possibly infected. You'll also see information on the master boot records and boot sectors scanned, as well as how long the scan itself took to complete. Now your system should be clean. If it needs to be cleaned, see the section on removing viruses earlier in this chapter.

McAfee's VirusShield

Chapter 5

What's In This Chapter

McAfee's VirusShield

VirusShield protects your system by scanning for viruses every time a disk or file is accessed. In Win 95 it operates as a virtual device driver, running in the background while you go about your other tasks in the foreground, scanning files and drives as you access them. In Win 3.x and DOS V-Shield works as a Terminate and Stay Resident in memory (TSR) program to protect you from viruses.

FEATURES OF VIRUSSHIELD

VirusShield works invisibly in the background while you go about your computing life, forming an invisible cloak of virus protection. It hunts for viruses each time a program is run, files are created, copied or renamed, or a disk is accessed or shut down. Some compressed files even have their interiors scanned by VirusShield. With a simple command line entered into your AUTOEXEC.BAT, VirusShield is activated when your system starts up. It can even prevent a warm boot from an infected disk. Really, the only way a known virus can get around VirusShield is if a component of VirusShield is disabled by the user or the system is started cold with an infected diskette in the drive. VirusShield should be your first line of defense against viruses.

Using/configuring VirusShield with Win 95

Being a component of VirusScan, VirusShield is installed when you install VirusScan, and the VirusShield icon will appear in the Win 95 taskbar. Double-click the VirusShield icon to open the VirusShield status window, which shows the last file scanned and statistics on the number of files scanned, infected, cleaned and deleted.

Open the status window now and you should see the last file you accessed listed under "Last File Scanned." Each time a file is opened, created, copied or renamed VirusShield inspects it for infection.

The status window has three clickable buttons. Clicking the [Disable] button will turn off on-access scanning. Next time you restart the computer it will automatically be reinstated or you can click the same button again. This has now been renamed [Enable]. The [Close] button will minimize the status window to its icon again.

Clicking "Properties" will open the VirusShield Configuration Manager window, which allows you to set how VirusShield will operate on your computer. These properties can also be edited through a text file in C:\Program Files\McAfee\Default.VSH (if you accepted the default locations during installation).

The VirusShield Configuration Manager has four pages with which you can work: "Detection", "Actions", "Reports" and "Exclusions". Use the "Detection" page to tell VirusShield what system areas to scan and when to run those scans.

To scan a file when it is created, copied, renamed or run, place a check in the appropriate boxes. Disks can be scanned each time they are accessed and/or when the computer is shut down. For the most complete protection, check each of these six fields.

What types of files do you want to scan?

"All Files" scans each file you use or you can set VirusShield to look only at program files. These are the ones most likely to be attacked by viruses. If you select "Program Files Only," click the [Program Files...] button to select the file extension types you want included in the scans of program files.

The (Default) button selects all executable program extensions. To remove an extension from the list, highlight it by clicking on it and then click (Remove). To add another extension to the list, click "Add" and enter the three-letter extension in the text field. Click (OK) when you are finished modifying the list of program files to be scanned. If you highlight "Compressed Files," LZEXE and PKLITE files will also be searched for viruses. The General parameters on the Detection page let you select whether the icon will appear in the taskbar, allow VirusShield to be disabled and set VirusShield to load when you start the computer.

If you remove the icon from the taskbar, you can access the configuration manager using C:\program files\mcafee\vshcfg32.exe. Some programs may require you to disable virus protection during installation, and will tell you so. Otherwise, there are very few reasons to disable VirusShield. For the most complete protection, load VirusShield at startup.

The "Actions" page is where you tell VirusShield what it should do when it encounters a virus.

You have five choices: "Prompt user for action", "Move infected files to a folder", "Clean infected files automatically", "Delete infected files automatically" and "Deny access to infected files and continue". The first option is the best choice for most users. It allows you to keep track of what happens in the computer and choose the best action for the particular instance.

The checkboxes select what options will be available to the user when a virus is detected. Unless you want to limit a user's actions, keep all of these checked. You can also select a message the user will receive when VirusShield discovers a virus. Check the box next to "Display message" and enter your bulletin in the text box. You may want to tell the user who to contact, or recommend an action to take.

If you choose to move the infected file to a folder from the Action page, enter the path and destination or use the [Browse...] button to locate the desired directory. It is also a good idea to restrict access to this folder or notify all users of its volatile contents so an unsuspecting user doesn't release the virus.

If you set VirusShield to automatically clean or delete an infected file, the action will be taken without directly notifying the user. If VirusShield is unable to repair the virus or doesn't have the necessary authority to delete a file, it will deny access to the infected file and notify the user. If you select "Deny access to infected files and continue," VirusShield will deny access to the file without direct user notification. This last option is recommended for machines that are left unattended.

The "Reports" page is where you can set up a log to record the scan activity. To create a log, click the box next to "Log to File:" and accept the default McAfee log or enter your own path and filename. You can also use the Browse... button to select a log file that already exists. You can set the maximum size of this log from 10 to 999KB. The bottom of the page lets you select the information you want recorded in the log.

The last page is "Exclusions". It informs VirusShield of items you don't want it to scan, either to save time or because you already know viruses are there (a quarantine folder, for instance).

To add to the list of exclusions, click the [Add...] button and enter the name of the file or folder to exclude. If you've chosen a folder, highlight"Include subfolders" to also exclude directories within the specified directory. Do you want this item excluded from file scans, boot sector scans, or both? Choosing both will cover all your bases, but "Boot sector" really only applies to disks. Click [OK] when you are satisfied with the exclusion. This same dialogue box will come up when you select an item in the exclusions list and click the "Edit" button. To take an object out of the list, highlight it with the mouse and use the "Remove" button at the bottom of the page.

When you've made all the changes you want to the configuration pages, click Apply to save the settings, or OK to save the settings and exit the configuration manager. Based on what you enter on these pages, VirusShield will intercept infected files in the computer and block others from entering your system. This almost invisible on-access scanning is possibly the best feature of McAfee's VirusScan. It provides a high level of security and ease of use.

VIRUSSHIELD FOR DOS AND WIN 3.X

In DOS and Windows 3.x, VirusShield operates as a DOS Terminate and Stay Resident in memory (TSR) program. It sits in memory and scans other programs and files as they are executed. Occasionally it will conflict with other TSR programs or with programs that monitor disk access. If you do run into problems, you can try running VirusShield with the /SWAP switch or use VShieldCRC instead (both of these options are explained later in this chapter.

VShield attempts to reduce conflicts by loading as much of itself as it can into high memory (extended, expanded and upper memory). If you have enough high memory available, VirusShield won't use any conventional memory (the first 640 KB). If you have only a very limited amount of memory, you can use the /SWAP switch to load an eight KB kernel of VirusShield into memory and load the rest of the program into a disk file.

When VirusScan was installed, VirusShield was installed with it. During that process you were asked if you wanted to add a line to the autoexec.bat file that would automatically load VirusShield each time the computer was started or restarted. If you did not use this option or if VirusShield was disabled during your computing session, you can activate it by going to a DOS prompt, navigating to the VirusScan program files directory and entering "VSHIELD" followed by your desired options.

VirusShield has twenty-five options but many of them would conflict if you tried to use them together. There are general options, affecting the VirusShield program itself; memory options, which configure how VirusShield uses memory; notification options, which can be used to alert users to the discovery of a virus; target options, used to configure the scans; and validation/recovery options, which you can use with SCAN's or WScan's validation feature.

The five general VirusShield options are:

- ❖ /? or /HELP
- ❖ /NOREMOVE
- ❖ /RECONNECT
- ❖ /REMOVE
- ❖ /SAVE

These help you manage the VShield TSR program.

The five memory options can be used when you need to conserve available memory:

- ❖ /NOEMS
- ❖ /NOUMB
- ❖ NOXMS
- ❖ /SWAP [pathname]
- ❖ /XMSDATA

They will help you load various aspects of VirusShield into high memory or to a disk directory.

The three notification options can be used to respond to virus detection:

- ❖ /CONTACT [message]
- ❖ /CONTACTFILE [filename]
- ❖ /LOCK

5 McAfee's VirusShield

The first two will display a message when a virus is found; the last locks the system to prevent further spread of the virus.

The eight target options configure your scans:

- ❖ /ANYACCESS
- ❖ /FILEACCESS
- ❖ /NOMEM
- ❖ /ONLY [drive(s)]

- ❖ /BOOTACCESS
- ❖ /IGNORE [drive(s)]
- ❖ /NOWARMBOOT
- ❖ /POLY

Use these switches to target different areas of your computer for a scan.

The last four switches are used with VirusScan's validation and recovery codes (see the VirusScan chapter for more information on validation codes):

- ❖ /CERTIFY
- ❖ /AV

- ❖ /CF [filename]
- ❖ /EXCLUDE [filename].

For complete details on how to properly use these switches, refer to McAfee's VirusScan User's Guide.

If you are low on memory, VShieldCRC is another on-access virus-protection option. It's protection isn't as complete as VShield's, but it uses considerably less memory. VShieldCRC does not scan for virus signatures or prevent infection, but it will detect infections and notify you when it finds a virus. It finds viruses through changes in the validation codes, so you must run Scan with an option for adding validation codes before you can run VShieldCRC.

After this, run VShieldCRC with your choice of options:

- ❖ /? Or /HELP
- ❖ /CF [Filename]
- ❖ /CONTACTFILE [Filename]
- ❖ /EXCLUDE [Filename]
- ❖ /IGNORE [Drive(s)]

- ❖ /CERTIFY
- ❖ /CONTACT [Message]
- ❖ /CV
- ❖ /FILEACCESS
- ❖ /LOCK

96

- ❖ /LOGFILE [Filename]
- ❖ /NOUMB
- ❖ /REMOVE
- ❖ /NOREMOVE
- ❖ /ONLY [Drive(s)]

Many of these are the same as those described for VirusShield. If you want to know more about using these switches, please consult the McAfee VirusScan User's Guide.

The one operation that a fully-functioning VirusShield can not protect you from is starting your computer with an infected disk. Seventy percent of reported virus infections result from boot viruses. When a disk is booted, the computer goes immediately to the boot sector for instructions on how to start up or for the "Non-system disk or disk error" message. If a virus is in this boot sector, it infects the computer before anti-virus programs are able to load, even if the boot isn't successful. User awareness used to be the only precaution against this, but McAfee recently released BootShield, an anti-virus program for DOS and Windows 3.1 that will prevent boots from an infected disk.

BootShield is available from any of McAfee's download sites and requires a PC with a 386SX or better processor, DOS 3.3 or later, 512K of RAM and 2M of disk space. BootShield works by making a copy of a computer's boot area and replacing the original with "BootLock code," which prevents any further change to the boot area.

When a boot virus attempt to move into the boot area it will be automatically removed and the boot area will be instantly restored. Because BootShield prevents the boot area from being modified, you will have to uninstall it if you need to change the boot area or will install a program that does so during its installation.

You may reinstall BootShield afterward. See the Whatsnew.txt for instructions on uninstalling. If an attempt is made to modify the boot area while BootShield is installed, the user is immediately notified and should use VirusScan to clean the infected diskette or program carrying the infection.

BootShield Installation

Before beginning installation, make a clean, blank formatted diskette. If you are in Windows, exit to DOS. Insert a disk that is blank or can be erased into drive A: and type "FORMAT A: /U" (without quotes). When prompted, enter a title for the diskette.

Now use PKUNZIP to unpack the zipped file if you downloaded it from a network.

Once the file is extracted, install and specify the source files. For instance, if the BootShield zip file was extracted to the TEMP directory on the C: drive, you would type "INSTALL C:\TEMP" at the DOS prompt to install BootShield into the current directory.

After a caveat screen, you will be asked if you want to continue installation. Type "Y," for yes.

If this is the first time you are installing BootShield, press "Y" again when prompted. If you are upgrading a previous installation, follow the directions on the screen.

The BootShield install program will check your computer's memory and system files and scan for viruses. You wouldn't want to protect an already infected boot area, after all.

BootShield will next be ready to create a clean boot disk for your computer. Insert the disk you formatted into drive A: and press "C" to continue. A bootable diskette will be created, including system and driver files. Leave this diskette in the drive during installation until you are directed to remove it. Afterward, be sure to label, write-protect and store this disk in a safe place. You may need it to uninstall BootShield.

Would you like ImageStor to create a backup of your hard drive at this time? Doing so requires you to have a second hard drive, an available network drive or an additional storage medium, like a tape drive or external disk drive. Refer to the BootShield documents for more information on ImageStor.

BootLock's setup program will launch now. You can access this program later by running the BSSETUP.EXE program.

Select the **File/Install** command.

Enter a name, company name and disk ID and note the paths BootShield is using.

After entering the necessary information, select "Start Installation."

Highlight "Yes" and press return when asked to confirm installing BootLock on your drive.

When told that BootLock installation was a success, follow the directions to restart the computer and remove the disk from drive A:.

After your computer is restarted you can run BSSETUP.EXE to check BootShield's status. The **Settings** menu lets you see which areas BootShield is guarding. The default areas include the master boot record, DOS boot sector and floppy diskette boots. You can also manage BootShield's messages from this menu.

Status, in the **File** menu, provides a concise report of where BootLock is active. Use the Uninstall command if you need to remove BootShield. You will need to do this if you want to change the boot sector or install another program that needs to do so.

BootShield detects and eliminates 99% of known boot viruses, including stealth, multipartite, polymorphous and encrypted viruses.

As you can see, McAfee has a several products that provide on-access scanning to protect your computer from boot sector, file and multipartite viruses. Because they operate in the background and load automatically at start up, they are very easy to use while providing a high level of protection. If you have any further questions about McAfee's on-access scanning products, visit their website or call McAfee Customer Care(www.mcafee.com and 408-988-3932, respectively).

WebScan
And Other
Internet
Protection

Chapter 6

6

What's In This Chapter

WebScan And Other Internet Protection

The Internet has brought everyone who uses it into virtual contact with an amazing amount of people. And when these people pass files back and forth they stand a chance of picking up an infected file. McAfee's WebScan will protect you from Internet borne viruses. It scans E-mail attachments and download files for viruses before they have a chance to infect your system. Executable and MS Word files, the predominant carriers of Internet viruses, are scanned even if they are inside a zipped file. WebScan integrates with the most popular World Wide Web browsers and E-mail programs. If you don't have Internet access or E-mail, SPRY mosaic browser and Pegasus E-mail are included in the WebScan package.

FEATURES OF WEBSCAN

WebScan provides automatic browser recognition during installation. It has a broad virus database and the same excellent support options as other McAfee products. Best of all, it operates transparently, automatically scanning files when you download without having to be separately loaded or otherwise called on.

6 WebScan And Other Internet Protection

Installing

Whether you are going to install WebScan from retail floppy disks or from a file you've downloaded from McAfee, the procedure is the same. Close any open programs first. Then run SETUP.EXE from the A: drive or from the directory where you saved the download. The setup program will prepare an InstallShield Wizard to automate most of the installation.

Click Next>. Select the type of installation that best fits your system's configuration.

A typical installation requires the most space and installs all the components of WebScan, including a tutorial and some example files.

A compact installation will install all of WebScan's elements except for the tutorials and examples.

A custom installation allows you to choose which components to install. Custom installation is recommended if you already have a browser and/or E-mail program. Choosing "typical" or "compact" installation will overwrite existing dialer programs and may affect other related programs as well. If you are using a Windows 3.1 system with an existing dialer and Internet connection, do not select a compact installation. If you do, WebScan will install its own dialer and Internet connection without asking you, overwriting existing files in the process.

After choosing the type of installation and the directory to which you want WebScan installed, click [Next>].

If you selected a custom install, the next page lets you choose which elements you want installed. Highlight a component to read a brief description of it. Mark the check box to select it. At the bottom of the page you can see the disk space required by your selections and the space that is available on your disk.

Choose the folder in which you want WebScan's program icons located. This determines in which folder the icons will appear in the **Start/Programs** menu.

Click [Next>]. Setup will scan for installed browser applications. Select the browser(s) which you want WebScan to safeguard and click [Next>].

You may have to update your AUTOEXEC.BAT file to complete the installation. If so, the installation wizard will prompt you to let it do so.

The next page lets you double check the settings you've selected.

Click [Finish] to complete the installation.

If WebScan doesn't recognize your browser during the setup procedure, then you will have to manually link the browser to WebScan.

First, launch the browser.

Netscape Navigator

In Netscape, select "General Preferences" from the "Options" menu and go to the "Helpers" tab.

Create or edit entries for executable files and compressed files. Make certain to link the following extensions to WebScan:

❖ .ARC	❖ .ARJ	❖ .BIN	
❖ .COM	❖ .DLL	❖ .DOC	
❖ .DOT	❖ .EXE	❖ .SYS	❖ .ZIP

Some of these extensions will already have associations. For those that do, select them in the window and then configure the action. For those that don't, click on the [Create New Type...] button. Then and create an entry for the following:

❖ Application/octet-stream (Mime type: application; Mime subtype: octet-stream)

❖ Application/octet-string

❖ Application/x-msdownload

❖ Application/msword

❖ Application/x-zip-compressed

❖ Application/zip

Then individually highlight each of these types and proceed to configure the associated actions. Select "Launch the application" as the action and enter the full path to the WebScan program in the blank, plus the switch "/SAVE". For example:

```
C:\PROGRA~1\MCAFEE\WEBSCAN\AV\WEBSCAN.EXE   /SAVE
```

After linking all of the file types to WebScan, exit and relaunch Netscape to save the new settings.

To confirm your installation with Netscape Navigator, launch Navigator and open the **Options/General Preferences** window and click the "Helpers" tab. If you linked WebScan to Navigator manually then you were just here. Manual or automatic linking, you should now see WebScan associated with program files. When you download one of these file types, the WebScan logo will appear and you will be prompted for a saving location.

For Microsoft's Internet Explorer, select the **View/Options...** command. Then "File Types".

Click [Create New Type...].

Enter a description (i.e., WebScan) and the list of file extensions. Click the [New] button to enter the action associated with these file types.

Enter a name for the "Action" such as "Scan". Then enter the path for WebScan's program file followed by the "/SAVE" switch, for example:

```
C:\PROGRA~1\MCAFEE\WEBSCAN\AV\WEBSCAN.EXE  /SAVE
```

Click OK twice and exit Explorer. WebScan should be enabled when you restart Explorer.

CONFIRMING INTERNET EXPLORER INSTALLATION

Restart Explorer and turn to the File Types page of Explorer's options and scroll the window until you see the description for WebScan you entered earlier.

At the bottom of the page you should also see the associated file types and program.

Navigator and Explorer are the two most popular browsers, but are certainly not the only ones available. If you have another type of browser, use its documentation to find out how to associate helper programs and use these instructions for linking WebScan manually. The procedure will be similar to that used with Navigator and Explorer, but the details will differ.

NOTES ON USING WEBSCAN

After installation, WebScan epitomizes ease-of-use operation. You do not need to load it or otherwise activate it. When you download a file recognized by the browser as one associated with the WebScan helper application, the browser automatically launches WebScan, which scans the file before saving it to your hard drive. That is all there is to it. You may now download anything from anywhere and WebScan will filter it (as long as WebScan is programmed to launch for that file extension). While you keep WebScan's virus database up to date, your system will be safe from Internet-borne viruses.

If you cancel a download in progress, WebScan may launch and scan the partial file. After scanning, don't save the partial file.

Using Navigator or Explorer, right-clicking on a file's hypertext link and selecting **Save Target As** won't call WebScan to scan the file.

Due to a small configuration problem, the SPRY dialer may display a Fatal Dialer Error if you click its shortcut from the Start menu. You can solve this by using the SPRY switcher to change from a LAN-based connection to a PPP or SLIP connection type.

Notes for Netscape Navigator users

Netscape 2.x saves downloads to a temporary directory defined on the "Apps" tab of Netscape's General Preferences (accessed from the Options menu). Navigator 3.0 saves downloads to the Netscape\Program directory. WebScan receives its path from Netscape and, after scanning the file, opens a Save As... box with this same path. Choose another directory in which to save the downloads, because all files in this directory are deleted when Netscape closes.

If a save is canceled, due either to a virus being detected or a user request, the temporary file is deleted to prevent infection. This may cause some problems when using the browser to access local drives. Just relaunch the browser to work-around this.

Notes for Internet Explorer users

Using Explorer, double-clicking a file's link to download it and selecting "Save It to Disk" will bypass WebScan. Choose "Open the File" to launch WebScan. You may then save it via WebScan's "Save as..." dialogue box.

In Explorer version 3.0 you won't be able to view source code. If you select View/Source, WebScan's flash screen will appear, but the source code will not be displayed.

Now you're set to safely explore the web and download whatever looks interesting. If a virus is contained in a download, WebScan will detect it and interrupt the download, thus protecting your system from infection. You may abort the download or continue and attempt to clean the file with VirusScan before opening or running it.

You can further protect yourself with other products, like WinZip 6.2 and the EZ Download plug-in, that have been designed to work with virus protection software. These are stand alone products that make aspects of using your computer easier. As part of this goal, they have been created to integrate their features with popular virus protection products, helping each product to protect you better than either could alone.

WinZip

WinZip 6.2 is a zipping/unzipping utility. One of the new features of this release is the ability to mesh with your virus protection software. Install WinZip according to the instructions in Chapter 1. If you are new to WinZip, take some time to explore its features with the tutorials available through the **Help** menu. On some system configurations, WinZip will automatically link to your anti-virus software. Others will have to manually configure the link. Open the "Program Locations..." window from WinZip's **Options** menu.

If your anti-virus program is listed in the "Scan program:" field, then WinZip has already recognized your scanning software. If not, see if your scan program is listed in the pull down menu.

If so, click it. If not, enter the program in the box.

When you open an archive in WinZip, you can scan it by selecting Virus Scan from the **Actions** menu.

You can also enable a virus scan when using WinZip's CheckOut feature, which lets you test out files before permanently saving them.

Open an archive in WinZip by selecting **File/Open Archive...** or clicking the (Open) button. Select the **Actions/Virus Scan** command. WinZip will activate your scan program and run it against the files in its archive. If you're using McAfee's VirusScan, the main VirusScan window will open and scan the files. If no infected items are found, VirusScan will tell you so.

When you close the VirusScan window, WinZip will tell you that the scan operation is complete. If any viruses are found, the VirusScan program will tell you before you return to WinZip. If you try to return to WinZip before the scan is complete, WinZip will prompt you to return to the scan or stop waiting for it to finish.

If you entered your scan program manually on the "Program Locations..." page and your scanner did not launch when you selected Virus Scan from WinZip's Action menu, return to the "Program Locations..." page and enter the full path to your scanning program.

Most files on the Internet are compressed to make transferring files easier. In order to use these files, you need to be able to unzip them. This is WinZip's primary function, but only one of its components. WinZip has many features that make working with zipped files easy and convenient, and the automatic link to VirusScan is more than a simple convenience; it's a safety feature for your computer.

EZ DOWNLOAD

Some people find the numerous steps involved in downloading a file from the Internet to be hassle, if not downright confusing. To automate your downloads, use the EZ Download plug-in. It requires your system to have PKUNZIP and either Netscape Navigator 2.0, Internet Explorer 3.0, America OnLine 3.0 or later versions of these browsers. EZ Download can automatically unzip and install .zip and .EXE files. It also supports Internet-enabled anti-virus software, launching the scanner during the download. After copying EZ Download to your computer, and unzipping it if necessary, run SETUP.EXE to install the plug-in. When prompted, click "Yes" to install. After installing, double click the EZDOWNLOAD.EXE file and enter the path for WEBSCAN.EXE in the field under Anti-Virus Scanner.

WebScan And Other Internet Protection

Once configured, EZ Download will perform all the tasks associated with downloading for you, and with your scanner loaded will scan the contents of any file you download. It will also install programs you download. You may configure EZ Download to do this when the file is downloaded or you can use EZ Download to install it at a later time by right clicking on the file and selecting EZ Install from the pop-up menu.

EZ Download makes downloading from the Internet and installing the downloaded files a snap. It's helper application status makes it incredibly easy to use, as it launches and performs most of its tasks automatically. The built-in link to WebScan means that infected files will be intercepted before they are saved to your system. With ease of use and a system secured against viruses, EZ Download lets you enjoy the Internet without worrying about its potential to spread viruses.

DOWNLOADING WALKTHROUGH

This short tutorial will take you through the process of downloading from the World Wide Web with WebScan installed as a helper application for your browser. Many of the steps can be automated if you use the EZ Download plug-in. We will use the Abacus's Web site for this demonstration but the process is the same from any Web site.

Step 1

Open your Internet access and launch your browser.

Step 2

Go to the Abacus Web site at www.abacuspub.com.

Step 3

Click the "Free Software" hypertext link.

Step 4

Select an item that interests you. At the time of writing the selection includes airplanes one may use with Microsoft's Flight Simulator, stereogram examples and demonstration, utilities and PC tricks. The site is updated frequently, so there may be a different selection when you visit. For this example choose a file type for which WebScan is configured to launch, like one of the airplane .ZIP files.

Step 5

To launch WebScan and begin downloading, click the hypertext link.

Step 6

WebScan will load and scan the zipped file. If it is free of viruses (and we at Abacus sure hope it is) WebScan will open a "Save the file as" dialog box. Select where to save the file and a name to save it as. Click OK.

You have just downloaded a virus-free zipped file from the Web. This procedure will be the same for almost any file you download. If you receive an "Unknown File Type" message from your browser during a download, your browser does not have an association entered for files with that extension. If you received this message during the walkthrough above, WebScan isn't properly installed in your browser.

WebScan And Other Internet Protection

The Internet and Word Wide Web have certainly contributed to the spread of file-infecting and macro viruses. But you don't have to worry about that, if you have WebScan installed on your system. Using WinZip and EZ Download makes working with files from the Internet very easy, and once they are linked to WebScan you needn't be concerned about infected files coming from the Web. WebScan combined with VirusScan provides the most secure system you can have from viruses short of disabling your communication ports.

Important Viruses & How To Contact McAfee

What's In This Chapter

Important Viruses & How To Contact McAfee

VIRUSES YOU SHOULD KNOW

The list of viruses in this chapter is by no means complete. This chapter will introduce you to some of the viruses that are most likely to infect your system and a few of the other well-known viruses that are not so much of a threat. Because boot sector viruses account for the majority of infections, many of these will be discussed. Macro viruses continue to be a growing threat, and so the latest and most widespread of these will also be discussed, as well as file and multipartite viruses that you may encounter. Before we get into those, lets talk about threats to your time and energy, but not to your computer: virus hoaxes.

Virus hoaxes

A virus hoax is a warning about a virus that does not exist. These hoaxes pose no threat to any computer and warnings about these viruses can be safely ignored. Some of these claim that the "virus" is being spread through E-mail. This is currently impossible. Viruses may reside in documents attached to E-mail, but none can travel in E-mail itself. If you do receive an infected E-mail attachment, you can still read the E-mail. The virus in the attached document is dormant until the document itself is opened (in a word processor, for example). To prevent an infection from an attached document, simply scan it before opening or executing it.

121

If you receive a notice about a potential virus, there are hoax characteristics for which you should look. Most hoaxes try to make themselves credible by using technical, but meaningless, language and associating the letter with an official or official-sounding organization. Follow up these sources before forwarding a warning.

A number of prominent hoaxes mention FCC warnings about a virus. The FCC does not, nor will it, issue warnings about computer viruses or trojans. It's not their job. Many hoaxes claim that the virus warned against is "virtually undetectable."

Almost all viruses give themselves away in some fashion. A virus would have to be both novel and very complex and advanced to be "virtually undetectable." While a genuine warning may have some of these characteristics, very few official statements encourage you to "pass this warning to your friends."

If you receive a virus warning over the Internet, look for these features in the warning, and don't pass the warning along unless you have some confirmation that the virus is real.

A moment of silence...

The warning about a virus contained in E-mail messages bearing the subject line "A MOMENT OF SILENCE..." is spurious. It warns against a mythical virus that can destroy your hard drive when you simply read the message. It talks about a new form of virus "unparalleled in its destructive capability." Hyperbole is another cue that a warning is false. Partial text of the original message follows:

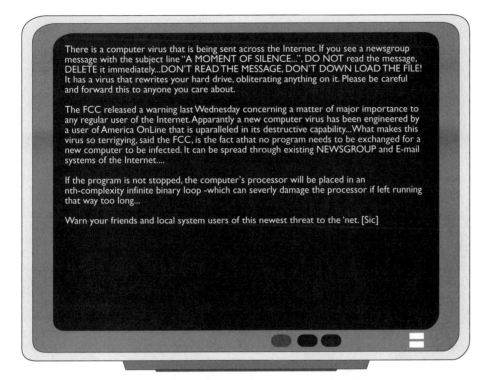

There is a computer virus that is being sent across the Internet. If you see a newsgroup message with the subject line "A MOMENT OF SILENCE...", DO NOT read the message, DELETE it immediately...DON'T READ THE MESSAGE, DON'T DOWN LOAD THE FILE! It has a virus that rewrites your hard drive, obliterating anything on it. Please be careful and forward this to anyone you care about.

The FCC released a warning last Wednesday concerning a matter of major importance to any regular user of the Internet. Apparently a new computer virus has been engineered by a user of America OnLine that is uparalleled in its destructive capability...What makes this virus so terrigying, said the FCC, is the fact athat no program needs to be exchanged for a new computer to be infected. It can be spread through existing NEWSGROUP and E-mail systems of the Internet....

If the program is not stopped, the computer's processor will be placed in an nth-complexity infinite binary loop -which can severly damage the processor if left running that way too long...

Warn your friends and local system users of this newest threat to the 'net. [Sic]

This message has almost all the hoax cues. The "nth-complexity infinite binary loop" is an excellent example of nonsensical technical language. The FCC never released such a warning. And a valid warning should encourage you to contact someone in authority or with knowledge of computers or the virus, not "anyone you care about." Spelling and typing errors are another indication that a notice may not be official.

Deeyenda

Deeyenda appeared in November of 1996 with the following message:

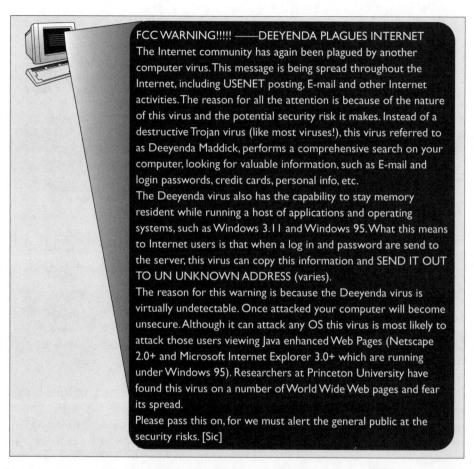

FCC WARNING!!!!! ——DEEYENDA PLAGUES INTERNET
The Internet community has again been plagued by another computer virus. This message is being spread throughout the Internet, including USENET posting, E-mail and other Internet activities. The reason for all the attention is because of the nature of this virus and the potential security risk it makes. Instead of a destructive Trojan virus (like most viruses!), this virus referred to as Deeyenda Maddick, performs a comprehensive search on your computer, looking for valuable information, such as E-mail and login passwords, credit cards, personal info, etc.
The Deeyenda virus also has the capability to stay memory resident while running a host of applications and operating systems, such as Windows 3.11 and Windows 95. What this means to Internet users is that when a log in and password are send to the server, this virus can copy this information and SEND IT OUT TO UN UNKNOWN ADDRESS (varies).
The reason for this warning is because the Deeyenda virus is virtually undetectable. Once attacked your computer will become unsecure. Although it can attack any OS this virus is most likely to attack those users viewing Java enhanced Web Pages (Netscape 2.0+ and Microsoft Internet Explorer 3.0+ which are running under Windows 95). Researchers at Princeton University have found this virus on a number of World Wide Web pages and fear its spread.
Please pass this on, for we must alert the general public at the security risks. [Sic]

Again we see a bogus FCC warning, an attempt to establish credibility ("researchers at Princeton") some techy language describing an invisible virus ("virtually undetectable") and an exhortation to spread the "warning" to the general public.

Irina

The last two examples were deliberate hoaxes, apparently done for the sake of the prank. Irina is as much an example of bad judgment as it is an example of a hoax. Guy Gadney, former head of electronic publishing at Penguin Books, sent notice of the bogus Irina virus to the media as part of a misguided promotion for a book of the same name. He neglected to include on the notice that this was part of a promotion and so the alert was passed to the computer community at large.

3222 2 2 2 2 2 2 2 2 2 2 2 2 2 2 2 2 2 2 2 2

Important Viruses & How To Contact McAfee 7

The notice was ostensibly sent from an Edward Pridedaux at the College of Slavic Studies in London, a character of the book. After researchers failed to locate any real Irina virus, and after the legitimate London School of Slavonic and East European Studies received many phone calls on the subject, the true nature of the "virus" was revealed.

Mr. Gadney is now breeding Idaho potatoes on an isolated hillside farm. (I don't know that for sure, but he isn't selling books for Penguin anymore either.)

Ghost

The GHOST.EXE "virus" is another example of bad judgment. Ghost.exe is a screen saver program advertising the author's company (Access Softek). It has a Halloween motif with ghost flying around inside a window. On any Friday the 13th, the ghosts are released from their window and allowed to roam the whole screen.

Well, one user panicked when the ghosts left their confinement, and without checking with anyone, sent out messages warning of a virus in the program. Just like the telephone game played at slumber parties, each time the message was passed on it became a little more distorted, until the rumor claimed that the Ghost "virus" would permanently damage a user's hard drive.

The end user's error in judgment created a community panic and many headaches for the authors of the original program, whose phone numbers were published in the program. Instead of checking with the authors, or reporting a possible virus to a virus research center, someone sent out a message reporting a virus that was picked up by others who embellished and passed it on further. Remember, even a little common sense can go a long way towards preventing problems.

If you think you've found a virus, please act responsibly. Copy an infected file or two to a blank floppy and then clean your system with an anti-virus program. Then contact McAfee, the Computer Incident and Advisory Capability (ciac.llnl.gov), or another virus research center. If they want a sample, you can send them the disk on which you placed an infected file. More likely than not, they will already have a sample or will explain that what you found was probably not a virus. If you receive a virus warning, consider the points made above regarding its authenticity, and seek some confirmation before passing the warning on the others.

MULTIPARTITE VIRUSES

Multipartite viruses are double-barreled, infecting both files and boot sectors in one shot. Because of this, their spread is wider than single point-of-infection viruses and they can be harder to clean out. The complexity inherent in being mulitpartite also limits their creation. There are plenty of these viruses, but not as many as of the other types. Scan all new files and diskettes to protect against these viruses.

Coup.2052

Like other multipartite viruses, Coup.2052 can infect your computer as either an infected file or an infected boot. You can catch it from a disk when you try to boot the computer from a disk that is infected with Coup.2052. Coup.2052, and other boot viruses, hide in the boot sector of disks, the area the computer reads to determine if the disk is bootable. By the time the computer decides if it can boot from the disk, a virus in the boot sector will have already infected the computer. You can catch Coup.2052 from an infected program by running the program. Coup.2052 infects .EXE and .COM files, and the master boot record of the hard drive, as well as the boot sector of any floppy disks accessed while the virus is resident in memory. Coup is also able to corrupt some DOS anti-virus programs, replacing them with the text:

Coup De Main: In Childhood taught me to Love, Now that I Love Frenzied, Said me Forget!!!

The most obvious indication of Coup.2052's presence is that infected files grow between 2,052 and 2,075 bytes. It becomes memory resident at the time of infection, and will become so each time the system is started until it is purged. It is a common virus that was identified in August of 1996. It has no currently known variants or aliases.

Junkie

The Junkie virus, also called "Junkie-1027" and "Junkie Boot," came from Malmö, Sweden, in May of 1994. It is a memory-resident encrypting virus that infects .COM files, diskette boot sectors and the master boot record.

When your computer is infected through an infected file, Junkie infects the master boot record and disables the DOS VSafe anti-virus TSR program. It won't infect files or become memory resident until the system is booted from an infected disk. Then it will move into memory and begin corrupting executed .COM files. It will also infect the boot sectors of diskettes that are accessed. The Junkie.1308 is a destructive strain of the virus, formatting sectors of the hard disk and displaying the following message:

Junkie shows itself by increasing the size of infected files by between 1,030 and 1,042 bytes. The DOS CHKDSK command will also show a loss of 3,072 bytes of available and total memory. McAfee rates Junkie as a common virus.

Markus.5415

Markus.5415 has it all: it's polymorphic, it encrypts itself, it uses stealth techniques and it goes resident into memory. Once on board a computer it will infect the master boot record and .EXE files. This rare virus came from Germany in September, 1996. It is fairly big, adding about five K. to infected files.

When triggered, Markus.5415 displays the following message (in German):

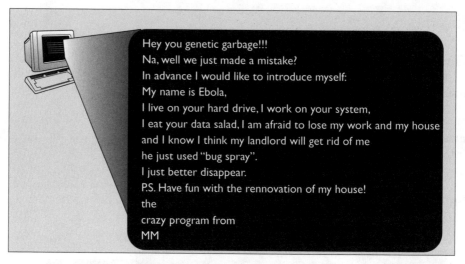

It then erases CMOS, slowly turns off the screen and reboots the computer. It also erases the partition table, so an infected master boot record can't be recovered with the DOS FDISK/MBR command. And on the 20th of May it displays "TYPE Happy Birthday Markus."

FILE INFECTING VIRUSES

File infecting viruses modify .EXE and/or .COM files. Whenever you receive a new program you should scan it for viruses before running it. If a file does contain a virus, that virus is dormant until the file is executed, when the virus replicates and infects other files.

2kb

Two Kilobytes, identified in October, 1994, attacks both .COM and .EXE files. It uses stealth techniques to hide its size, which is two kilobytes. Symptoms of this virus are increased size of infected files and file allocation errors when running DOS CHKDSK, as well as a decrease in system memory. Most AV programs can clean 2KB from your computer.

Butterflies

Identified in June of 1993, Butterflies only infects .COM files and does not go resident in memory. When you run an infected .COM file, Butterflies will infect all the other .COM files (between 121 and 64,768 bytes) that are in the same directory, including read-only, hidden and system files (but not COMMAND.COM). It increases the size of infected files by 302 bytes and will sometimes hang your computer when you run an infected program. This virus may be of Italian origin, as it contains Italian text, as well as the encrypted English text "Godd—n Butterflies."

Dark Avenger

Suspected to be of Bulgarian origin, Dark Avenger was identified in September, 1989. It is a malicious, memory resident virus that infects all .EXE, .OVR and .COM files whenever they are executed while Dark Avenger is in memory.

This virus also stores a counter in the hard disk's boot sector. After each sixteenth file is infected it will overwrite a random sector of the hard drive. Anything that was in an overwritten sector becomes unusable.

Dreamer.4808

The Dreamer.4808 virus infects .COM files and stays resident in memory to infect more .COM files. It also hides by using stealth strategies. It appends itself to the end of the legitimate files, increasing their size by 4,808 bytes each. This virus was signed "Hitler Virus by Dreamer/Dy" which gives it both its name and its alias, "Hitler." This version was found in August, 1996, and has one known variant, Dreamer.8869.

Rescue.911.3774

Rescue infects .EXE files and does not stay in memory. It is a common virus with no known variants, discovered in October, 1996. Files infected by Rescue.911.3774 grow by 3,774 bytes.

If you run a validation scan when Rescue.911.3774 has changed a file, the virus will display this message:

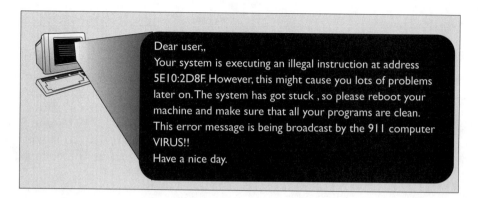

Dear user,,
Your system is executing an illegal instruction at address 5E10:2D8F. However, this might cause you lots of problems later on. The system has got stuck , so please reboot your machine and make sure that all your programs are clean. This error message is being broadcast by the 911 computer VIRUS!!
Have a nice day.

MACRO VIRUSES

Macro viruses are a new and quickly growing class of viruses. They infect the documents of programs that utilize a macro language, and spread quickly because most users don't scan these types of files. Read chapter three for details on protecting yourself against macro viruses, and scan documents you receive from others before opening them.

Alien.macro

Alien is a common macro virus that infects Microsoft Word .DOC and .DOT files. When it infects Word files it brings "AutoClose," "AutoOpen" and "FileSaveAs" macros with it, which it uses to spread and infect other documents. It will also remove TOOLSMACRO and TOOLSCUSTOM from the Tools Menu. When the user exits Word, Alien displays one of the following randomly selected messages:

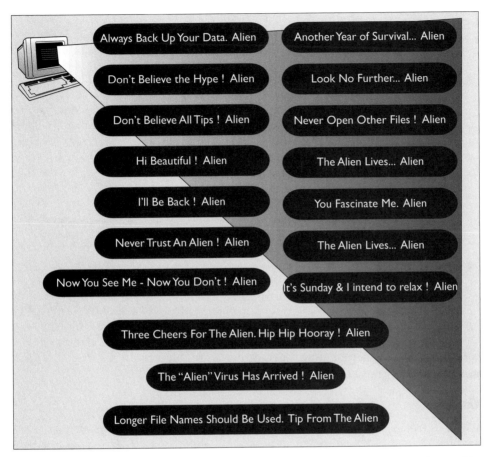

Always Back Up Your Data. Alien

Another Year of Survival... Alien

Don't Believe the Hype ! Alien

Look No Further... Alien

Don't Believe All Tips ! Alien

Never Open Other Files ! Alien

Hi Beautiful ! Alien

The Alien Lives... Alien

I'll Be Back ! Alien

You Fascinate Me. Alien

Never Trust An Alien ! Alien

The Alien Lives... Alien

Now You See Me - Now You Don't ! Alien

It's Sunday & I intend to relax ! Alien

Three Cheers For The Alien. Hip Hip Hooray ! Alien

The "Alien" Virus Has Arrived ! Alien

Longer File Names Should Be Used. Tip From The Alien

Alien is believed to have originated in the United States and was catalogued in October of 1996. It is also known as Chandi, with no known variants.

Concept

This was the first macro virus, an unfortunate trend setter. Concept is a common and particularly widespread macro virus because it was accidentally shipped in two popular CD-ROMs. It is American in origin, first identified in July, 1995, and is dependent on English versions of Word.

It infects documents and the NORMAL.DOT template. When Concept is introduced to a new system, it searches for the Payload and FileSaveAs macros. If either is found it aborts infection, believing the system is already infected. If these files don't exist it will display a small dialogue box bearing the message "1."

When the user clicks the [OK] button the virus activates, replacing the FileSaveAs command with its own and copying its AAAZFS, AAAZAO and Payload macros. You can see these macros on an infected machine in Word's **Tools/Macro...** menu. It also causes infected documents to behave as templates. Concept is not destructive. The Payload macro contains the message:

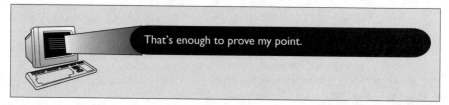
That's enough to prove my point.

Concept has a number of variants: Concept.B:FR, Concept.C, Concept.D, Concept.E through Concept.I. It is also known as Prank, WinWord and WWW6Macro. As of April, 1996, Concept was reported in over a dozen countries and was responsible for roughly 25% of all worldwide reported virus infections.

Gangsterz

Gangsterz is another language independent Word macro virus which infects .DOT and .DOC files. It activates on January 15th. When a new document is opened on this date, Gangsterz prints

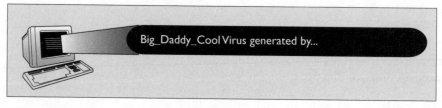
Big_Daddy_Cool Virus generated by...

This gives it it's alias, "Big Daddy Cool," or "BDC." Infected documents contain Gangsterz and Paradise macros. It was identified in October of 1996 and behaves like other Word macro viruses.

Laroux

Laroux uses the macro language of Microsoft's Excel spreadsheet program. It infects .XLS files with "auto_open" and "check_files" macros. It does not appear to be widespread, but has infected some companies's databases and is classified as a threat by the National Computer Security Association. Laroux isn't designed to destroy data (it contains no payload), but it may because of bugs in the program that prevent it from running as smoothly as it was intended to run.

NPad

Discovered in August of 1996, NPad infects Word .DOC and .DOT files. When it infects a document file, the AutoOpen macro appears in the Tools\Macros... menu. After infecting 23 files NPad displays a series of message boxes announcing its origin (Indonesia) and a copyright notice. NPad is also known as WM.Jakarta and is considered a common virus.

Wazzu

Wazzu, originating from the U.S. is an interesting and annoying macro virus. It also uses the AutoOpen macro. This is a popular macro for viruses to take advantage of because it is the same in all language editions of Word. This macro allows a virus to infect documents as they are opened. Each time an infected document is opened Wazzu executes a routine that has a 20% chance of randomly rearranging up to three words in the document, and another routine that has a 25% chance of inserting the word "Wazzu" somewhere in the text. Variant "F" also displays an additional text string: "EAT THIS: This one's for you, BOSCO." There are six known variants of this virus: Wazzu.A through Wazzu.F.

BOOT INFECTING VIRUSES

Boot viruses are few in number compared to all viruses, but are responsible for most infections: around 70%. While there are a number of anti-virus programs that can catch most viruses, very few can prevent you from booting your computer from an infected disk, the medium through which boot viruses are passed. When starting your system, be sure that no disks are present in the floppy drives, and scan every disk before introducing it to your system. If your computer contracts a boot virus, power the computer off and restart from a clean startup disk.

Air Cop

Air Cop is a memory resident boot sector infecting virus out of Taiwan. It was discovered in July of 1990, and manifests characteristic virus symptoms: system hangs, strange messages and a decrease in total and available memory. It is not intentionally harmful, but may corrupt some diskettes and the hard drive may become unbootable due to imperfections in the programming.

When it infects a diskette it will copy the original boot sector to another location on the disk. If data is later written to this location, the boot record is lost. While memory resident, Air Cop will infect the boot sector of any floppy disk that is accessed. Sometimes it will display:

RED STATE, Germ Offensing—Aircop

Alameda

The Alameda virus was identified in 1987, making it one of the oldest viruses, and now has many variants. The original Alameda contains no harmful programming, but some of its variants are quite malicious. It replicates at warm boots with the Ctrl+Alt+Del key combination and loads itself into memory. At the same time it will try to circumvent a warm boot by intercepting the command, blanking the screen, beeping and moving drive heads to simulate a warm boot. It will also infect accessed floppy disks.

Variants include Golden Gate (which can reformat your C: drive) and SF. Because this virus has been around for a while it is well known to most anti-virus programs and is rare in the wild.

AntiCMOS

Initial infection of the AntiCMOS virus occurs when a computer is booted from an infected diskette. At this time the virus infects the hard drive's master boot record. When the computer is restarted from the infected hard disk the virus will move into memory and infect floppy diskettes used on the system. You may also notice problems during the boot process and a decrease of roughly 2,048 bytes of memory.

If not removed promptly, AntiCMOS will overwrite the system CMOS, which contains setup information for the computer. Since its discovery in 1994, AntiCMOS has spawned three variants, AntiCMOS.A, AntiCMOS.B and ANTICMOS C. It's also known as LiXi because of an internal text string: "I am Li Xibin!"

AntiEXE

This malicious virus is believed to have come from Russia in late 1994. When the computer is booted from an infected diskette, the virus attacks the master boot record and becomes resident in memory. Once active, the virus hides by relocating the original boot sector or master boot record. If you attempt to view the boot sector or master boot record, the original will be displayed.

If the Ctrl+Break key combination is pressed while the virus is accessing the disk it will begin overwriting the disk. It also hunts and corrupts .EXE files of 200 or 256 bytes. Diskettes are also vulnerable to AntiEXE. Memory decreases by 1,024 bytes on an infected system.

Also known as Stoned, this is one of the more common boot viruses. Its other aliases are CMOS4, NewBug and D3. As of April, '96, this virus was responsible for about 9% of reported infections worldwide.

ASBV

Known since October of 1996, ASBV is a memory-resident boot virus that employs stealth and encryption techniques. It is common and may make the hard drive unbootable. It goes into memory after infection and infects floppy disks from there, erasing sectors. ASBV has two text messages:

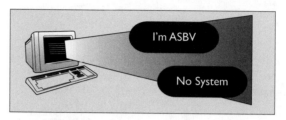

A new virus, it does not yet have any variants.

Azusa

Hailing from Hong Kong, Azusa moves into memory upon infection. From there it will infect any floppy to which you write data. It overwrites the boot sector and master boot record and may disable LPT1 and COM1 ports. Azusa reduces memory by about 1024 bytes. It was identified in January, 1991.

Cansu

Identified in June, 1992, Cansu moves into memory when the computer is infected. The first time the master boot record is accessed after infection Cansu will move into the master boot record. It will also infect accessed floppies. Cansu evades detection with polymorphing characteristics. After 64 diskettes are infected on a machine Cansu displays a "V" on the screen.

Dir-II

Dir-II comes from Bulgaria and was identified in September, 1991. It is a memory-resident boot-infector that also targets the directory structure. It infects .EXE and .COM files during read/write operations with the sectors containing information on those files, infecting all executable files within the directory. It encrypts the pointers for the executable programs and orients them to itself, so the size of the files doesn't change and only one copy of the virus needs to be on any machine.

When one of these programs is called for, the command is directed to the virus which executes the program. You won't notice any ill effects until the machine is restarted, when the directory structure is corrupted. Dir-II may indicate its presence with cross-linked files and data corruption when you try to copy a file. Its stealth abilities even allow it to evade most anti-virus shields.

Form

Coming from a high school student in Zurich, Switzerland, in the summer of 1990, Form is a non-malicious memory-resident boot virus. It does not damage data on the hard drive, but may corrupt diskette contents. When it infects the boot sector of a hard disk, it relocates the original boot sector to another area of the hard disk. If data later overwrites this sector the system may hang during booting.

Form has two main symptoms. On the 18th day of any month, each keystroke produces an audible click. This may not be noticeable if a keyboard driver is used. On the 24th of any month it creates a delay when keys are pressed. You will also notice a loss of two K of memory when you run the DOS MEM command to check your memory.

The binary virus code also contains a message:

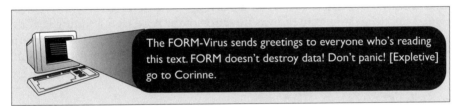

It has a number of variants and aliases, all of which contain "Form" in the title. Form is responsible for about 17% of reported world wide infections.

Michelangelo

Michelangelo activates on March 6th, reformatting the hard disk and overwriting all data in the process. It moves into memory and infects the boot sector when the computer is booted from an infected diskette. It reduces total available memory by 2,048 bytes. Michelangelo is dangerous, but well known (identified in May, 1993), and can be detected and cleaned by most anti-virus programs.

Monkey

This stealth, encrypting memory resident virus is known since October of 1992. Monkey moves into memory the first time the system is booted from an infected disk. It encrypts the master boot record and moves it, taking residence in its place. It then directs calls to the MBR to the new location. It will also infect floppy disks accessed while it is in memory and may corrupt the diskette directories.

Until the virus is cleaned from the computer, trying to access the C: drive after booting from a clean disk will summon the message "Invalid drive specification." Monkey also has a number of variants and aliases, all variations on "Monkey" (because all versions contain the encrypted word "Monkey").

NYB

At infection, NYB infects the master boot record and memory, from where it also infects accessed diskettes. This virus does not display any messages at start up, and uses stealth strategies to hide its infection of the hard disk, making it difficult to notice. System memory will decrease by 1,024 bytes. It may also cause errors when formatting or accessing floppy diskettes. It was discovered in January, 1995. It has no variants, but two aliases: B1 and Stone.i.

Stealth_C

Stealth_C is a full stealth virus, infecting the master boot record, diskette boot sectors and residing in memory. Because of its well-developed stealth abilities, be sure it is not resident in memory before scanning the hard disk or floppies. If it is in memory, it will hide infections from the scanning software. Stealth_C may disable 32-bit disk or file access and will interfere with memory management, preventing some drivers from loading and creating problems running Windows. It uses 4,096 bytes of memory.

This virus is from the U.S. and appeared in January 1995. Its variants include the Stealth_Boot series and it is also known as Amse, Nops.B, Stelboo and PMBS. It is very rare in the wild.

Updates, Forums and Contact
INFORMATION

Virus protection software is only effective when it is contemporary with extant viruses. Over 100 new viruses appear each month, and if your anti-virus software has gone a while without being updated, it may not be doing you much good.

Therefore, McAfee provides 90 days of virus-data files updates for all registered owners of Single-user Retail anti-virus products. These updates will keep your anti-viral software appraised of the latest viruses, helping you to keep them out of your system and if they should infect you, helping you to clean them. These are usually updated monthly and each data file update hunts between 60 and 150 new viruses.

These updates are available from McAfee's Web site, FTP site, CompuServe, America OnLine, The Microsoft Network and the McAfee BBS. Download the zipped file to your system, scan it with WebScan or VirusScan to make sure that it is uncompromised, unzip the file and copy the contents of the zipped file to the VirusScan and/or WebScan folder. These files will overwrite the previous data files and protect your system against recently discovered viruses.

If you purchase one of McAfee's anti-virus software packages and a new version is released within ninety days of your purchase, you are entitled to a onetime free upgrade online. To update your product(s) within 90 days of purchase, contact McAfee's Customer Care department (408-988-3832 (telephone) or 408-970-9727 (fax)) to receive a log-in and password to McAfee's registered user area.

Technical support is available to registered and evaluation users twenty-four hours a day, seven days a week through their online channels. This includes forums on CompuServe, AOL, and MSN, files from the BBS and FTP site, their World Wide Web site and an automated voice and fax system.

Free telephone assistance is also available between six and six (pacific time) Monday through Friday on a line devoted to home users only.

Registered users can also sign up for optional maintenance plans. For maximized protection, McAfee offers a one year online maintenance and support package that entitles the user to a full year of product upgrades and updates, as well as electronic, online and telephone support services. Alternatively, you can keep up to date without downloading by joining the One Year Quarterly Disk/CD Maintenance and Support Program, which offers a quarterly mailing of diskettes or CD (depending on the product) and a quarterly newsletter, each of which will help you stay on top of current virus outbreaks.

McAfee's website also has encyclopedic information on important viruses. There are a number of other web-based virus centers as well. Using any search engine will return a host of databases. Some you may want to check out for more information on a specific virus or viruses in general include: the Computer Incident and Advisory Capability (ciac.llnl.gov), the National Computer Security Association (www.ncsa.com), the AVP Virus Encyclopedia (www.avp.ch/avpve) and www.antivirus.com, the "Most Comprehensive Online Source of Computer Virus Information."

Contacting McAfee

By telephone

To contact McAfee, use one of their Customer Care department telephone numbers:

408-988-3832 (Monday-Friday, 6:00 AM to 6:00 PM (PST))
408-970-9727 (24-hour fax)
408-988-3034 (24-hour fax-back automated response system)

By mail/snail mail

You can also use the following "snail mail" addresses:

McAfee Corporate Headquarters
2710 Walsh Avenue
Santa Clara, CA 95051-0963

McAfee East Coast Office
Jerral West Center
766 Shrewsbury Avenue
Tinton Falls, NJ 07724-3298

McAfee Central Office
5944 Luther Lane, Suite 117
Dallas, TX 73225

McAfee Canada
178 Main Street
Unionville, Ontario
Canada L2R 2G9

McAfee Europe B.V.
Orlyplein 81 - Busitel 1
1043 DS Amsterdam
The Netherlands

McAfee (UK) Ltd.
Hayley House, London Road
Bracknell, Berkshire RG12 2th
United Kingdom

McAfee France S.A.
50 rue de Londres
75008 Paris
France

McAfee Deutschland GmbH
Industriestrasse 1
D-82110 Germering
Germany

By online assistance

The following table lists the sites and services where you can contact McAfee:

Bulletin Board System	408-988-4004 (24-hour US Robotics HST DS
Internet e-mail	support@mcafee.com
Internet FTP	ftp.mcafee.com (205.227.129.134)
World Wide Web	www.mcafee.com (205.227.129.97)
America Online	keyword MCAFEE
CompuServe	GO MCAFEE
The Microsoft Network	GO MCAFEE

Frequently Asked Questions

Chapter 8

8

Frequently Asked Questions

Q **What is the real virus threat to me?**

Computer viruses should not be ignored by anyone who uses a computer. However, the actual threat to your computer depends on how you use it. Each time you introduce a new disk or program to your system you risk an infection, and so people who frequently share disks are at more risk than someone who rarely does. Downloading files from the Internet or world wide web can also bring a virus into your system. So while everyone is at risk, some are more so than others. Everyone's risk is negligible if he or she takes simple precautions to protect his or her system. Learning about viruses and running anti-viral software are easy to do and the best precautions for every computer system.

Q **VirusScan found a file but says it can't be cleaned. What do I do?**

First, be sure you are using the most updated virus database. An updated database may have the tools to clean an infection that an earlier database could only detect. If your data files are current and you can't clean the virus, you'll have to use VirusScan to delete the infection. You may try to remove it yourself, but there is a good chance that some of the virus hiding in the corner of some obscure program will be missed. Run VirusScan again after it removes the virus to be certain that all of it was removed and your computer is safe to restore the

145

lost files. After removing the infected files with VirusScan you may replace them with clean backups from a write-protected disk. If the virus was found on your hard drive or master boot record you will have to restart from a clean boot disk and then remove it with VirusScan.

Q	What does "Evaluation version" mean?

An evaluation version allows you to run a program through its paces before deciding if you want to buy it. Many evaluation versions provide the full features of the registered version. After using the program for a limited time, usually thirty days, you should register with the authors of the program or remove it from you computer. The evaluation versions of VirusScan and WebScan included on the CD-ROM let new users learn about the benefits of using McAfee's virus protection software and to follow the examples in the book. McAfee granted us permission to provide these evaluation versions at no cost to you so you may preview their features and abilities. If you like what you see and will continue to use the programs after thirty days, please register with McAfee to receive the full benefits of their support, including ninety days of virus updates and the option of receiving continuing updates and support.

Q	I'm a comparison shopper. What other anti-virus packages should I look at before deciding which is right for me?

There are a variety of other products out there, ranging from comparable to poor. McAfee's VirusScan boasts a twenty percent better detection rate than their nearest competitor and one of the largest virus laboratories. Two other leading anti-virus packages are from Norton-Symantec and TouchStone Software Corporation. Norton's Anti-Virus supports DOS/3.1, Win95, Win NT, Macintosh, Novell and Netscape platforms and applications. TouchStone's PC-Cillin has gotten good reviews and is also available on a number of platforms. More information about both of these can be found on the web, as well as other products that protect home users against viruses.

Q	What are the differences between VScan, VShield and WebScan?

VirusScan provides on-demand scanning with the ability to detect and remove most known viruses. See chapter four for a complete discussion of VirusScan's features. VirusShield is a component of VirusScan that operates in the background, scanning for viruses each time you access a new disk or execute a program, without you having to give it an explicit command each time. See chapter five for a complete description of VirusShield. WebScan protects against viruses transported across networks, including the Internet and world wide web. It operates as a helper program for your browser and scans files when you download. If one of the files you want is infected with a virus, WebScan will notify you before it can infect your system. See chapter six for more details about WebScan.

Q	How can I catch a virus?

You can catch a virus from accessing or booting from an infected diskette, executing an infected program, or working with an infected data file. You should always use anti-virus software when you introduce a new item to your computer to prevent an infection.

Q	If I catch one, how can I get get rid of it?

The surest way to remove a virus is with virus-cleaning software. Viruses can be removed manually, but unless you are an expert, the results are bound to be haphazard. If one of McAfee's products notifies you of a virus, use VirusScan to clean it. Some files are infected beyond repair and must be deleted to prevent further spread of the virus.

Q	How can I get the most recent version of one of McAfee's products?

We've included the most recent version that was available at the time of printing. However, viruses are continually evolving, and the anti-viral software is adapting to the changing viruses. To get the most recent versions of McAfee's anti-virus programs, download it from their website, BBS or FTP site. If you've registered, you have ninety days to contact McAfee and receive a onetime free update to the latest version.

> **Q**   I always use anti-virus protection software before introducing anything into my computer system. My neighbor never uses an a-v program. Am I paranoid or is he foolish?

An ounce of prevention is worth a pound of cure. Your virus protection needs depend on how frequently you introduce new programs and files into your computer and where they come from. You must consider how you use your computer, how valuable its contents are and how valuable is the time you would spend repairing and replacing programs that would be lost if an unprotected computer were to become corrupted by a virus.

> **Q**   What is the absolute best method to prevent viruses and maintain a practical system?

Again, this answer depends on how you use your system. For most users, education and an anti-virus program that prevents, detects and cleans viruses will protect without interfering. Combining VirusScan and WebScan creates a secure virus protection scheme that operates almost invisibly and combats over 96% of the viruses that are in the wild.

> **Q**   Can I catch a virus by surfing the Internet?

You can not catch a virus by browsing the Internet or world wide web. Web pages themselves can not carry a virus into your system. You may pick up an infected file in a download. Even then, the virus will not be activated until the file is accessed or the program is executed. Scan every file you download before using it. Or better yet, use WebScan to catch viruses as they download.

> **Q**   My computer acts strangely sometimes. Is this a virus?

Most likely not. Computers are complex machines performing millions of complex functions, and while generally reliable, they are not perfect. Most of the things that go wrong with computers are in no way related to viruses. But because viruses are themselves so complex and varied, there is no simple list of symptoms that can be ascribed to a virus infection. If your computer acts strangely all of a sudden when you haven't changed anything in the system, you may have a virus. Whenever you suspect a virus may be in your computer, run your scanning software.

> *Q*   I frequently get virus alarms, but there is no evidence of an actual virus.
> What's going on?

If you are using validation codes as part of your VScan or VShield scans and are getting false alarms, you probably have a program or hard disk that uses self-modifying code. The alarms are genuine in that the validation codes perceive the program has altered, but the cause is not a virus. Identify the items that are repeatedly causing the alarms and include them in the validation exceptions list to avoid future false alarms from these programs.

> *Q*   How do viruses avoid detection?

Viruses try to avoid your detection with innocent titles, like the AOL Gold trojan horse, which tries to fool users into thinking it is the latest release of America OnLine's browser. Noone would download a file named DEATHVIRUS.EXE. Viruses try to avoid your anti-virus's detection by either encrypting themselves or polymorphing. Encryption viruses encode themselves so that other programs won't recognize them for what they are. Polymorphous viruses evade detection by changing their form. They are made of pieces of code that can be rearranged into any order and still execute properly. This way each infection is unique (within a range of possibilities) and the virus won't be tracked by a signature string of code. However, VirusScan utilizes a heuristic scanner which can detect even tiny pieces of signature code, which allows it to catch most polymorphous viruses.

> *Q*   Where do all these viruses come from?

Some viruses have been released on accident or as experiments gone awry. Most are deliberate, either intentionally malicious or as an annoying but relatively harmless statement by the author, declaring his or her programming expertise or pointing out security flaws on networks. Some programmers design viruses for the challenge of evading detection and spreading as far as they can—instead of designing a better mousetrap, they are creating better mice. (And if you're paranoid, there's a theory that viruses are released by the same people who sell anti-virus software, creating a perpetual market for themselves. But that's only if you're paranoid.)

> **Q** What do I do with a corrupted file?

A corrupted file is one that is damaged beyond repair. If it is on your computer, delete it with VirusScan and restore it from a clean backup copy. If it is on a floppy disk you may also delete it or, if it is the boot sector of the disk itself, you could use it as a coaster, a square frisbee, cut another eyehole and use it for a mask. . .

> **Q** I was warned about the Good Times virus. Is it particularly dangerous?

Good Times is not a computer virus but a social virus. The actual virus never existed, but a near panic was created by false rumors about a virus traveling in an attachment to an E-mail with the subject "Good Times." The false rumors were fed to the Internet and then users started passing it along without verifying it, creating an escalating alarm over nothing. If someone warns you about a virus over the net, particularly someone you don't know, ask where s/he got the information.

> **Q** How can I find out about the most recent viruses?

There are many resources for virus information on the web. McAfee's website is a good place to start, as well as the National Computer Security Association (www.ncsa.com) and the Anti-virus Center (www.antivirus.com). A complete list of viruses in the wild is available at www.virusbtn.com/WildLists/index. Others include the Computer Incident and Advisory Capability (ciac.llnl.gov), the AVP Virus Encyclopedia (www.avp.ch/avpve) and www.antivirus.com, the "Most Comprehensive Online Source of Computer Virus Information." Using any search engine will return a host of databases containing virus information.

> **Q** How often should I scan my system?

This also depends on you use your system and how frequently you introduce new items into it. A computer with a lot of traffic may need to be scanned daily, but most home users will be safe with a weekly or monthly scan. Whatever schedule you use, it is important to have a regular schedule for your scans, which you can also coordinate with a regular schedule for backing up your files. Backing up after a scan is a good idea because you know you have a clean system to backup.

> **Q** I have the evaluation version of VScan. Can I copy this for a friend?

Read the license agreement with your version of the evaluation copy for specifics from the owners, but most evaluation copies are freely distributable on a small scale. If you do pass it along, your friend is bound by the same rules of usage as you are. If he or she likes the product and will continue using it beyond thirty days, that person should register.

> **Q** I have a registered version of VScan. Can I copy this for a friend?

No.

> **Q** VirusScan found a corrupted file and I don't have a backup. How can I restore my file?

Sorry. If it was particularly valuable information it may yet be recoverable, though the effort and expense may be considerable. Call McAfee's Customer Care department to learn about your options.

> **Q** As part of my plan for world domination, I want to introduce a virus into the world's computers that will give sole control to me. Can you tell me how to write such a virus?

No. And if I could, I wouldn't. I can't spend my time helping world-domination wannabes. I barely have enough time to concentrate on my own plans for ruling the world, the last thing I need to do is foster competition.

> **Q** Are all viruses harmful?

By definition, a computer virus attaches to a host program, and this is almost always harmful to the host, damaging data or creating execution errors. Not all viruses are malicious, but all do at least a little damage.

> **Q** Are viruses a real threat, or is this another example of fear-mongering media?

If you protect yourself with education and an anti-virus program, and if everyone else did the same, viruses would pose almost no threat to you at all. As it is, with computers controlling so many aspects of everyday life, from banking to shipping to communication to utilities and many other areas that are

151

often taken for granted, a strategically placed virus with enough ingenuity could wreak havoc in most major cities. However, those in charge of the important computers are also aware of the risk viruses pose and have taken steps to protect them that are much more stringent that anything you or I have on our computers. To be brief, the answer is "Yes" to both questions.

Q | Can viruses travel through a LAN (local area network)?

Macro viruses and file infector viruses can and do travel through local area networks. Boot sector viruses are restrained to traveling via floppy disks.

Q | How do I make backups of my materials?

First scan your system to make sure that it is free of viruses. There is no sense in making a backup of anything containing a virus. Then simply copy the contents of your computer onto floppies or, better yet, a tape drive or other external storage medium.

Q | What is a boot disk, why do I need one, and how do I make one?

A boot disk contains the commands your computer needs to start itself up. If your computer's boot sector or master boot record were ever to become infected, you would need a clean, write-protected boot disk to start your system cleanly and remove the infection. The steps for making a boot disk are detailed in chapter three.

Q | Is VirusScan supported on any other platforms?

In addition to DOS, Windows 3.x and Windows 95, you may also get VirusScan for OS/2, Windows NT, Solaris and Macintosh.

Q | I keep getting a message that my data files are out of date. What do I do?

If you are a registered user of VirusScan, virus database updates are available from any of McAfee's download areas. Once you have the update, just copy the files into the directory containing the current program and data files. The new update will overwrite the old data files.

Q	How do I register with McAfee?

You may register with McAfee through the mail, over the phone or electronically at their website.

Q	During installation, I'm asked if I want to modify my autoexec.bat. That's a serious step, isn't it?

It is, but a safe one to take. What it will do is add a line to load VirusShield at startup so that virus protection is enabled from the beginning, without you having to load it each time you start the computer.

Q	My Windows 3.x or DOS system hung up when I rebooted after installation. What's up with that?

You may have a TSR conflict between VirusShield and another memory resident program. To determine if this is the cause of the system hang, reboot from a diskette and remark the VirusShield line in the autoexec.bat. To do this, go to a DOS prompt after rebooting, and add "REM" before the line that loads VirusShield. Reboot the system again from the hard drive. If it still hangs, the problem is not with VirusShield. If it does boot you should edit VirusShield's command line in autoexec.bat. Remove the "REM" command and add the following switches to the end of the line: /NOEMS, /NOXMS and /NOUMB. Try them individually, and then in combinations, rebooting between each configuration. These switches determine how VirusShield works with expanded, extended and upper memory, respectively.

Q	When installing WebScan, the wizard failed to find my browser. How do I link the two together?

Chapter six details the manual installation process for Netscape Navigator and Microsoft Internet Explorer. If you have another type of browser, the steps will be similar, though the details will be different. If your browser is so different from these that the instructions in chapter six aren't helpful, read your browser's manual for information on linking helper applications or plug-ins to the browser.

Frequently Asked Questions

	When I try to download from the internet, WebScan launches but doesn't save the file.
Q	

You probably installed WebScan to your browser but did not include the "/ SAVE" switch at the end of the command line. See chapter six for more details.

Glossary Of Anti-virus Terms

Chapter 9

Glossary Of Anti-virus Terms

Behavior blocker

Some virus detectors monitor the activity within a system. When they notice a suspicious command, they interrupt to verifying that the user, not a virus, is making changes to the system.

Boot

To boot is to start a computer. During startup, the computer loads instructions from a disk's boot sector. A warm boot is when your system is restarted by pressing reset or the `Ctrl`+`Alt`+`Del` key combination. This restarts the OS, but does not clear the memory. A cold boot occurs when the system is powered down completely and then turned back on. This method clears any contents from memory.

Boot sector

A disk's boot sector contains the information for booting an operating system and explains to the computer how the disk should be read.

Boot sector virus

Attacks the boot sector of a disk. These are especially dangerous because data in the boot sector gets loaded into memory before an anti-virus program can be run. A "true" boot sector virus attacks only the boot sector, no matter whether the target is a hard drive or a floppy. Some viruses always infect the first physical sector of the disk, no matter what type of disk.

Bug

An error in the programming or assembling of soft- or hardware that causes the item to not operate as intended. Bugs range from being so minor as not to be noticeable to halting all system operations.

Clean startup disk

This is a write-protected, uninfected floppy diskette containing the instructions a computer needs to boot. If your system catches a boot sector virus, using a clean startup disk is the only way to eliminate it.

CMOS

The CMOS (Complimentary Metal-Oxide Semiconductor) chip is also known as the BIOS (Basic Input/Output System) chip. By either name, it is responsible for retaining essential system hardware configurations that enable the PC to start up and operate properly.

Companion virus

A viral program which does not attach to another program by overwriting files. Instead it uses a similar name and rules of program precedence to link to a regular program. Companion viruses are also known as "Spawning" viruses.

Corrupted file

A file that has been irreparably damaged by a virus (though viruses aren't the only cause of file corruption). Ten to twenty percent of all virus infections damage files beyond repair.

Disinfect

To remove a virus from a system or file so it can no longer infect other files or disks.

Dropper

A "Dropper" is an executable file that is able to create a virus and infect a system when it is run. Virus scans do not detect a virus when a dropper program is scanned because the virus hasn't been created yet. The viral code is created when the dropper program is run.

Encryption

Encryption refers to the modification of data, code or files in such a way that users cannot read or access encrypted data without unscrambling (decoding) it. Viruses use concealing their code with encryption to avoid discovery. Encryption of code or data can also be an element of a virus's payload.

False alarm

A report of a virus when none is actually present.

File virus

File viruses bind or link themselves to files. They ordinarily attach onto the beginning or the end of a program file or else overwrite the code of the program. Often, we call programs "file viruses" that don't actually join themselves to files. Instead, they associate themselves with program filenames (see Companion Virus). In most cases, file viruses attack program files.

Integrity

The proper format and/or handling of data. Viruses attack the integrity of data when they seek to modify or erase program information or database entries in a file, for examples.

Logic bomb

A form of trojan horse, usually with malicious effect. Logic bombs are set to execute at a certain command, input sequence or change in a file.

Macro virus

Some large applications use macro languages to automate repetitive tasks. Some macro languages offer the ability to write into files other than the original document. This feature may be exploited by virus authors to create virus macros which will reproduce and infect other documents that utilize the macro language. Macro viruses are known to infect and spread through Word and Excel files.

9 Glossary Of Anti-virus Terms

Master boot record/Boot sector virus

This virus attacks your computer hard drive's MBR (Master Boot Record) or a boot sector. The MBR/boot sector virus takes charge of your system at a low level, becoming active between the operating system and the system hardware. MBR/boot sector viruses are loaded into memory when you boot up your machine, before virus detection code gets a chance to run. Most infections occur from booting the system with an infected diskette in a disk drive.

Memory resident

A program that remains in the computer's random access memory (RAM) while other software is executing. These viruses are designed to infect other programs which access the memory.

See also Terminate-and-Stay-Resident.

Multipartite virus

Multipartite viruses attack master boot records, boot sectors and files.

Parasitic virus

Parasitic viruses overwrite information or code in a file. In the process, they contaminate or destroy what they overwrite. While virus cleaning software can usually remove the virus, it may not be capable of undoing the damage the virus does.

Payload

The payload is what happens when a virus is triggered, or set off. The payload could be something simple, such as a message or graphic appearing on your screen. However, it could also be something more complicated and damaging, such as contamination or deletion of data. The payload of most viruses is replication.

Polymorphic virus

This virus type tries to avoid discovery by altering its inner arrangement or its methods of encryption (encoding). Polymorphic viruses employ a technique of changing the appearance of the virus with each attack to evade discovery by virus detection software. They are able to do this because they are made up of several pieces of individual code. With each infection these pieces are rearranged into a random order, thus preventing the virus from having a signature string of code. Techniques that aren't quite as advanced are called "self-encrypting," where the structure isn't altered, but the encoding scheme is different with each infection.

Rabbit

A program created to exhaust a computer's resources by replicating itself without limit. Eventually the computer gets so tied up with replicating rabbits that it can't perform other functions. Rabbits do not infect other programs and so are not true viruses.

Rogue program

A term used by the press to denote any program intended to cause damage to programs, data, or security.

Spawning

A program that does not attach to another program, but links itself to another program by adopting a similar name and usage protocol. See Companion Virus.

Stealth

Refers to the different methods viruses employ to prevent discovery.

Stealth techniques include redirecting system pointers to infect a program without actually modifying its code, and creating a masked image of a program for the system to look at instead of the actual file, thus hiding changes the virus has made.

System hang

When a system error occurs, the offending program usually has a chance to display an error message. If the error is serious enough, no message will be displayed and the computer will seem to freeze or lock, with no data going in or out. Some times the system can be retrieved by pressing the [Ctrl]+[Alt]+[Del] keys together; other times you'll have to power the computer off and restart.

Terminate - And - Stay resident (TSR) program

A TSR program stays resident (active) in memory when other programs are running. Examples of TSRs are hardware drivers and anti-virus programs.

See also Memory Resident.

Time bomb

A trojan horse with a time-based trigger. It may be set off at a certain time, on a particular date, or after being on a system for a set amount of time.

Trigger

The trigger is the occurrence for which the virus has been programmed to wait before administering the payload. The trigger could be a date, series of keystrokes, the number of days since the virus infection took place, almost anything, actually.

Trojan horse

A Trojan horse disguises itself as a useful, or at least innocent program, but it comes with a harmful payload. Trojan horses aren't viruses in the strict sense of the word, since they don't replicate.

Variant

A variant is a new virus based on code from an older virus. While it shares code with the original virus, the variant usually incorporates one or more new characteristics and often enhanced stealth techniques.

Virus

A program that joins to another program. It then reproduces itself and attaches to another program, from where it continues the process of replicating and infecting. The effects of a virus range from displaying harmless error messages to crashing computers and destroying data.

Upper memory

This is the area between the conventional 640K of RAM and one megabyte (1024K). Many TSR programs will try to load into upper memory to keep conventional memory available to other programs.

Worm

A program that replicates itself through networked computers. These may be harmless, utilizing otherwise idle resources to perform operations in the background, or they may spread unauthorized, using up needed computing power and overloading a system.

Write protection

A means of keeping data from being written onto a diskette. When a diskette is write protected, it is immune from virus infections.

Index

166

Index

Index

169

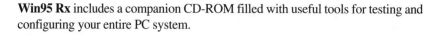

Multimedia Presentation

PC Photography Book

The PC Photography Book is for all camera buffs, home users, hobbyists, desktop publishers, graphic artists, marketing communication professionals and multimedia enthusiasts.

Many companies, including Kodak, Seattle FilmWorks, Storm Software, Delrina, Hewlett-Packard and others, are pioneering a new consumer level technology which lets you move common photos or snap shots onto your PC. Digital imaging software and graphic gear is easier to use, more affordable and the quality of output excellent.

PC Photography starts with the basics of image processing and taking quality photos. A special treatment is given to Kodak's photo CD format that allows anyone to put photos on CD-ROM. The technology and process are both explained in depth. It then moves on to examine how today's hardware and software work—both the digital camera and the photo reader.

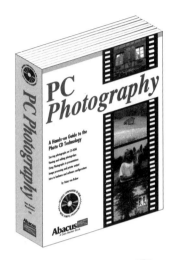

Includes CD-ROM with Sample Programs

Learn how to work with: Micrografx PhotoMagic, Microsoft Publisher, CorelDraw, Aldus Freehand and Photostyler, and Adobe PhotoShop.

The companion CD-ROM includes samplers of:

- Toshiba's Photo/Graphic Viewer
- MicroTek's Photo Star graphic utility
- PCD photo examples used in the book
- Collection of popular shareware graphics
  utilities including:
  - JASC'S PaintShop Pro
  - Graphics WorkShop
- Several industry standard Phillips CD-I software drivers

**Author: Heinz von Buelow
         and Dirk Paulissen**
Order Item: #B293
ISBN: 1-55755-293-2

**SRP: $34.95 US/$46.95 CAN
      includes CD-ROM**

To order direct call Toll Free 1-800-451-4319

In US and Canada add $5.00 shipping and handling. Foreign orders add $13.00 per item.
Michigan residents add 6% sales tax.

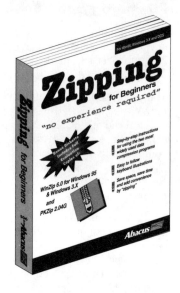

Software

ZIP KIT

Learn to Use the World's Most Popular Data Compression Programs!

Start Using WinZip and nine other fully functional evaluation versions of the most popular data compression shareware in the universe today.

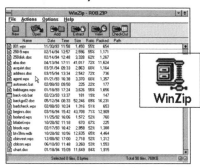

PKZip

ARJ

LH-ICE

PKLite

LHArc

LZH

This Windows-based utility makes unlocking the treasures of the information superhighway a breeze. Zip and unzip. Drag-and-drop. Virus scanning support.

Graphic & Video Utilities

Special graphic and video programs in the **ZIP KIT** will help you work with dozens of different formats.

Learn to convert and compress numerous graphic formats with unique image processing software: ART, BMP, DIB, GIF, IFF, ICO, LBM, MSP, PCX, RLE, TIF, WPG, CUT, EXE, HRZ, IMG, JPG, MAC, PIC, RAS, TGA, and TXT.

Discover the world of compressed video files: FLI, AVI, MPG, FLC, and MCI.

ZIP KIT
Item #S287   SRP: $34.95 US/ $46.95 CAN
ISBN 1-55755-290-8
UPC 0 90869 55290 1

To order direct call Toll Free 1-800-451-4319

In US and Canada add $5.00 shipping and handling. Foreign orders add $13.00 per item. Michigan residents add 6% sales tax.

Nets and Intranets With Win95
Getting Connected

Windows 95 has a surprisingly rich set of networking capabilities. Built-in networking delivers an affordable and easy way to connect with others and benefit by sharing resources—files, printers, and peripherals. Network sharing saves you and your organization time and money and adds convenience.

Another great benefit of Windows 95 Networking is its ability to let you run an Intranet. This book and companion CD-ROM has all the pieces that you'll need to set up your own internal World Wide Web server (Intranet) without the expense of using an outside Internet Service Provider.

CD-ROM Included

- A practical hands-on guide for setting up a small network or Intranet using Win95 or Windows for Workgroups 3.11.

- Take advantage of Windows 95's built in options so you can immediately use its networking features—

  - Shared printers
  - Easy-to-use groupware
  - E-mail and faxes
  - Additional hard drive capacity
  - Centralized backups
  - TCP/IP

- Step-by-step guide to getting and staying connected whether you're in a small office, part of a workgroup, or connecting from home.

- Perfect for the company wanting to get connected and share information with employees inexpensively

Author: H.D. Radke
Item #: B311
ISBN: 1-55755-31-4
SRP: $39.95 US/54.95 CAN
        with CD-ROM

Order Direct Toll Free 1-800-451-4319

In US and Canada add $5.00 shipping and handling. Foreign orders add $13.00 per item.
Michigan residents add 6% sales tax.

Installing Acrobat Reader & McAfee Anti-Virus Evaluation Version

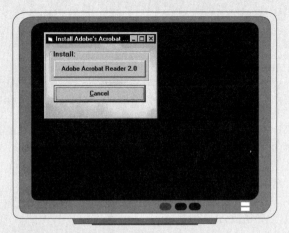

Companion CD-ROM Program Notes

Keep in mind, however, that shareware programs are copyrighted programs, not freeware. Therefore, the authors (McAfee & Associates, MMMMM Software, Inc. and Niko Mak Computing, Inc.) require payment if you continue using their program(s) after a specified trial period. This lets you try out the program for a limited time, typically 30 days, and should give you enough time to decide whether you want to keep the program. If you continue to use the program, you're required to send the author a nominal fee. Please read the README.1ST in this directory for instructions.

After registration you will frequently get the current full version of the program without restrictions and shareware notes, as well as the option of purchasing upgraded versions later for a reduced price. As a rule, larger applications include a users manual. Shareware programs usually feature the complete performance range of the full versions. Some programs use special messages to indicate they're shareware versions. The message usually appears immediately after program startup or can be called from the Help menu.

The companion CD-ROM shows the variety of shareware available. To ensure that the program authors continue writing programs and offering them as shareware, we urge you to support the shareware concept by registering the programs that you plan to use permanently.

You'll find program instructions and notes on registration for the shareware programs in special text files located in the program directory of each program. These programs are usually called READ.ME, README.TXT or README.DOC. As a rule, the TXT, WRI or DOC extensions are used for text files, which you can view and print with Windows 95 editors.

The MENU program is a component of the companion CD-ROM. It's not shareware, freeware or public domain. Please do not redistribute the MENU program from Abacus.

The Companion CD-ROM

To use the companion CD-ROM, you must first load the MENU.EXE program located in the root directory of the CD. When this program is loaded, you will have various buttons for selecting your utilities.

See Chapter 1
For Complete
Details

Insert the CD-ROM into your CD-ROM drive. For Windows 3.X users, select the **File/Run...** command in the Windows Program Manager. This opens the Run File window. Type the following in the Run dialog box:

```
d:\menu.exe
```

Press (Enter) or click the (OK) button. The main MENU program will start. This MENU program is used to install or test various shareware utilities.

For Windows 95 users, select the **Start** menu and then the **Run...** command. This opens the Run dialog box. Type the following in the Run dialog box:

```
d:\menu.exe
```

and press (Enter).

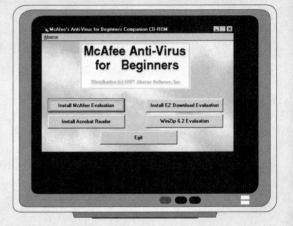

Installing Niko Mak Computing's WinZip and EZ Download

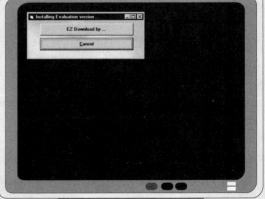